Contents

Backyard Memories, Front Porch Dreams

(and a few Semi-Exciting observations along the way)

Larry Cribb

Larry Cribb
Columbia, SC

To Joyce, Sharon, Laura, Rachael, Courtney and Allison,
the women in my life.
My fondest wish, which I offer with love, is for you to
always remember that good memories
are true treasures.

10 9 8 7 6 5 4 3 2 1

ISBN 0-9705151-0-3

Library of Congress Control Number: 00-092531

Book Design by Pam Whitmore and Susan E. Collins

Printed by Martin Printing Company, Inc., Easley, SC

ALSO BY LARRY CRIBB
How You Can Make $25,000 A Year With Your Camera
(Published by Writer's Digest Books)

Curious about the cover? See Chapter 3

Chapter 1

Backyard Memories

When I was growing up, my backyard wasn't a big place, but it was a very special place. It's been a long time, but I'd guess it was only about 75 feet wide and maybe 35 feet deep.

More important than its size, however, was the part it played in shaping my childhood experiences. It was the scene of hundreds of adventures—some real, most imagined. There I planted my first garden; ventured into the world of commerce for the first time; had my first medical emergency when I fell off a "little red wagon" and broke my arm; almost had my second, and possibly fatal medical emergency, when I let playmates hang me from the pecan tree.

We always had great neighbors on both sides, but the back of our lot was bordered by a coal yard—Skinner's Fuel Oil (and Coal.) Actually it helped make the backyard more of a private place. The only time I remember any of us venturing over the back wire fence and into the coal yard was once when my Daddy went turkey hunting over there!

That surprise you? Turkey hunting in a coal yard? Well, it was really all my fault. It was Thanksgiving and one of Daddy's insurance clients paid the past-due premium with a live turkey. We were going to have it for Thanksgiving dinner. We draped the turkey's neck over a big block of wood and Daddy was going to sever it while I held the bird in place.

Daddy raised the ax, the turkey flopped and I let go. The next thing we knew, the turkey had flown over the fence into the coal yard. Daddy got his double barrel 20 gauge, climbed the fence and went hunting. He was a bit miffed, but secretly I think he enjoyed the adventure. At least I hope he did. The turkey dinner was great.

Free Coal?

Coal was a big item back then for home cooking and heating. We used it mostly in the little cast iron heater in the kitchen that was connected to our hot-water tank. Not only did it provide us with hot water, but heated the kitchen. Of course, in the summer that really wasn't a big benefit.

We had a coal bin in the backyard that was usually at least half full. When I was a youngster, I sometime wondered why Daddy always paid for coal from Skinner's when all we would have had to do was reach through the fence and get all we wanted. I guess that was one of my first lessons in doing the right thing. My Mother and Daddy always did the right thing, and they expected their children to do the same.

The coal bin probably meant more to me than it did to them. Not only did it hold fuel, it also served as an army tank, a stage coach, a trench from which to fight the enemy, or just a place to get your clothes very, very dirty. There wasn't much of a way to deny that you'd been playing in the coal bin.

Playground Equipment

The backyard also contained some other playground equipment that lent itself to great adventures. There was a single tree, and it stood right in the middle of the yard. It was a pecan, but it very seldom, if ever, had any nuts on it.

It was, however, an excellent lookout tower and once almost turned into a hangman's tree. After the Saturday cowboy movies, several friends and a cousin would come by the house where we would recreate the action of the movie we'd just seen. On one occasion, I drew the lot of being the movie villain who had been hanged.

Cousin Edwin said we'd have to go through with the plot. I let them tie the noose around my neck and stepped up on the wooden box as they threw the rope over a limb of the tree. I really didn't think they would kick the box out from under me . . .

Do you know what a real rope burn feels like? It's no fun, but I guess it wasn't much compared to the broken neck I could easily have suffered. Anyway, I sported a rope burn on my neck for a few weeks. From then on, I always insisted on being one of the guys who wore the white hat.

There was another time when we re-enacted a cowboy and Indian movie. A couple of us had real, old hunting bows that people had given us. They were about 40-pound pull bows I believe, and we had metal-tipped target arrows. We wrapped tissues around the tips and secured them with rubber bands. Then we shot them at each other.

I guess what saved us in that adventure was the fact that we didn't have enough strength to pull the string back far enough to do any real damage.

Just Four Walls and a Roof

There was also a nondescript backyard building that was a combination storage room and garage. We never kept the car in the garage part, but it was always full of all kinds of good things to tinker with, and a place to play when it was raining.

At one time, the storage room housed a German military museum, which you'll read about later; became my first photo studio and darkroom; a hideaway where I could write stories; a store for my rummage sales and a club house where you could have real, private conversations with friends.

I also built a table out of plywood where I could lay out my electric train. Not having the benefit of a level, or enough legs to keep the too-thin plywood from buckling, I tried to explain to buddies that this was supposed to be a mountain layout so the train had to climb hills and go down into valleys. I never did figure out a way to keep it from tipping over, or keep the tracks from separating.

In keeping with our unusual childhood adventures, Cousin Edward and I decided the roof of the storage room would be a good place from which to take off and soar like a bird. We mounted the building, opened our umbrellas and leapt into the sky. The ground turned out to be a lot closer than we had imagined. Fortunately, this stupid adventure had a happy ending—no broken bones.

My First Business

To a youngster, this backyard, as small as it was, provided ample space for a never ending series of adventures. It was there I began my first business—raising chickens. I bought 25 pullets and sold the ones that didn't die in their infancy, and reached eating size, to neighbors. I made $15 on the deal. Daddy lost $29 on the same deal!

7

After that, I tried to talk him into letting me raise pigeons or rabbits to sell, but he flat put his foot down on those ideas.

The backyard was the place where I built my first sailing ship clubhouse out of cardboard cartons that had contained refrigerators, and a few appropriated boards.

It was here that I learned the great art of tree climbing, harvested my first tomato, took target practice with my air rifle and almost learned how to use a hammer and saw.

But most of all, I remember that when I was in my backyard, I was safe from the world. And I could pretend that it was anything or anywhere I wanted it to be. You'd be surprised at some of the distant places I visited in that cardboard sailing ship, or some of the wondrous sights I saw from high up in that pecan tree.

It's gone now. There's an automobile dealership built right smack dab on top of it, but it'll always be there in my memory. Sometimes today I think how nice it would be to have a place like that where I could retreat once in a while. But those retreats now have to be taken in my mind.

Did you have a backyard? I hope so. If you did, I'll bet you also have some great memories of that very special place.

Chapter 2

Never Sit on a Hot Spark Plug

I guess my first boat was a real pirate sailing ship. I built it in my backyard out of cardboard refrigerator cartons, a few pieces of lumber I salvaged from a neighbor, a small table and chair I appropriated from the house, and a candle holder.

The candle holder was probably the most important piece of equipment on the ship, for it held the light source that provided the illumination in the ship's hole where my friend Claude Kirkland and I operated the vessel on our many cruises across the world's oceans.

That sturdy ship was never in danger of sinking, in fact never did even spring a leak. Probably the main reason for this phenomenal accomplishment was because there was no water in our backyard. A borrowed piece of canvas kept the "marine" cardboard in pretty good shape during rainstorms—except when we forgot to cover it in late afternoon and it rained at night.

Shipyard Conversions

At one point, we converted this pirate vessel of old into a modern naval frigate, but it didn't have the same sense of adventure. Perhaps it was because a frigate is so big, didn't have any sails, and we never could appropriate any sure enough cannons.

From that, we next converted it into a World War II PT boat because we did have torpedoes. And a PT boat is much more romantic, faster and easier to handle.

On To Bigger and Better Floats

As I grew older, I graduated into a craft that would really float in wet water. It was a 12-foot, flat bottom, homemade beauty that some unknown builder made of plywood. Painted red and white, it boasted a power plant of a 5 hp Royal outboard motor.

The Sampit River that ran along Georgetown's Front Street, and

9

the creeks of nearby Pawleys Island were my domain as I skippered this plywood cruiser whenever I could afford money for a gallon or so of gas. I usually ran it dry on every trip. It would have been to my advantage if I could have afforded a set of oars. Instead when the need arose for self-power, I fell back on a hand-carved paddle my Granddaddy made out of cypress.

He liked cypress a lot better than plywood—used to make boats out of it himself. But by the time I was ready for one, he was out of the boat building business. His last boat that I remember was chained to a big cypress tree at Haselden's landing. There was a brass lock on the log chain.

Alas, Daddy and I hiked to the landing one day for some jiggerpole fishing. When we got there, all that was left was the chain—cut by what must have been a three-man bolt cutter.

Most of my boating was done alone. Claude trusted me completely to guide the pirate ship, the frigate and even the high-powered PT boat. PT boats, you know, have twin diesel engines that turn up hundreds, if not thousands of horsepower. But he never did learn to let himself go and enjoy the trip when I was at the helm of that 5 hp gasoline outboard on wet water!

Land Transportation Needed

When I decided I was more in need of land transportation, I traded this treasured and much-used craft. I traded with an older gentleman who lived at Pawleys Island for a Cushman Motor Scooter. He had seen me zipping through the marsh grass, dodging sand bars at low tide and occasionally scraping an oyster bed in the Island creeks. But I always stayed afloat. He wanted that boat, and I wanted his wheels.

"At my age, I need a boat more than I need a motor scooter," he mumbled when he approached me and asked if I wanted to trade.

For the first time in a long time, I was boatless. I had traded away my old red and white, flat-bottomed hulk, and the "marine" cardboard of the PT boat had finally succumbed to the elements.

But my landlubber adventures were much increased. Now I could fly low with the breeze in my hair, never have to wait for the family car to be available, be free to travel the highways and byways of Georgetown. Biggest problem with that was I had a crew cut, and that scooter never did reach the velocity necessary to make that hair wave in the breeze.

I don't know who got the best deal in this trade. I do remember that my Mother wouldn't let me drive the scooter the 12 miles on Highway 17 from the Island back to town by myself. She and my brother, Alan, followed me in the car.

I kept stopping to check with her on what the speedometer was reading as I opened the throttle. Don't believe we ever got above 17 miles per hour, but then the scooter did need a little work. It was supposed to do 35 mph.

A Budding, Sparking Mechanic

When we got home, I took the body off so I could get to the engine and begin a tune up. That consisted mainly of wiping away some grease and oil and putting in a new spark plug.

The hum of that powerful piece of equipment was music to my ears as I kicked the pedal and it sprang to life. I was overcome to the point where I jumped aboard in a standing position and opened it up as I circled the pecan tree that dominated our small back yard.

Now on this model, the spark plug stood upright directly under the seat cushion. The seat cushion was a permanent part of the body. In my exuberance, I seemed to have forgotten that I didn't replace the body of the scooter before I had cranked it up.

As I gained momentum circling the tree, it dawned on me that I would have more control if I changed to a sitting position rather than continuing to stand.

You guessed it . . . sat right down on that spark plug . . . which was not only a somewhat sharp and pointed instrument, but was also crackling with electricity as well!

Was quite a jolt to the posterior—so much so that the scooter continued in one direction while I went in another. I had to park the Cushman for a few days while I recovered and was able to sit once more.

I hammered out the few dents caused by the driverless scooter meeting the stationary pecan tree head to head. Cranked it up and found the engine hadn't suffered in the collision.

That was the last time I ever test-drove that scooter in a standing position. In fact, for as long as I had it, every time I took the body off to work on the motor, I had to overcome a cold sweat before I could make the necessary repairs.

Men Toys Cost More Than Boy Toys

As a grownup, I've had several boats from powerful, lightning-fast, bass-fishing machines to the little 14-foot fiberglass fishing vessel parked under the carport now. Guess this one will last me from now on.

In the Navy, I sailed on a Destroyer Escort as a NROTC Midshipman, and on the world's newest and biggest Aircraft Carrier at the time—the USS Ranger (CVA-61) as an Ensign (and later a LTJG.)

All my boats have been fantastic and contributed immeasurably to my enjoyment of the great outdoors. I've sailed the North Atlantic, been off Cape Hatteras in a storm as the boilers on our Destroyer Escort went out. I've cruised the Caribbean, the Gulf of Mexico, traversed the Panama Canal, rounded Cape Horn and traveled the Pacific from California to Japan.

I've fished such diverse bodies of water as Lake Erie, Lake Ontario, the Mississippi, White and Ohio Rivers. I've floated on Lake Murray, Dale Hollow, Lake Eufaula and countless others.

When it comes to land travel, probably nothing beats the two-wheel adventures. My Cushman Motor Scooter was a lot of thrills all wrapped up in a single package. It did teach me, however, never to sit on a hot spark plug.

I told the family that when I retired, I was going to buy me a real motorcycle. My Granddaughter said: "forget it Granddaddy. Keep your old two-wheel memories of that scooter. That's as close as you'll ever get to a motorcycle. Too dangerous at your age."

Whether on land or water, propelling on two wheels or floating in 12 feet of plywood, 14 feet of fiberglass or 1,046 feet of Navy gray steel, none of them provided the excitement or the adventure of that cardboard pirate ship which took Claude and me on so many cruises without ever leaving the safety of my backyard.

Chapter 3

No, it's Not a Sissy Bike

When I was a youngster, May Day was an important day. The entire town celebrated with a giant parade. It concluded with everyone, parade participants and spectators, gathering at the home of Mrs. Frank Turner on Prince Street.

She had a huge backyard where the First of May festival was held. The grounds were dominated by the tall May Pole erected in the center of everything. Long ribbon streamers were tied at the top and hung down the pole. As a climax to the celebration, beautiful young girls in long, wispy, pastel dresses would each take a streamer and intertwine as they danced around the May Pole.

The ribbons wound ever tighter until all of the young ladies were shoulder to shoulder at the base of the pole. It was quite an honor to be selected as a May Pole dancer.

There were food booths with homemade cookies, cakes and pies. There was real lemonade, hot dogs and hamburgers. Fishing booths, where youngsters fished for prizes, always had a long line, as did most of the other games. There were sack races and other activities for the youngsters—a day-long affair.

May Day was like a small-town, whole-town picnic.

The Parade

The local high school band led off and provided the music. There were floats, Boy Scouts, Girl Scouts, kindergarten groups, convertibles with beauty queens, dance schools, young majorettes, politicians and perhaps a military honor guard. Just about anybody with any possible excuse could join the parade.

From as young as I can remember, I was always in the parade. First, Mother decorated my little red wagon and I pulled that with my dog sitting in it. When I could ride a tricycle, she decorated that—crepe paper interlaced in the spokes of the wheels, ribbons on the handle bars and the seat and flowers everywhere.

Later she decorated my tri-bike, a large three-wheeled

combination tricycle and bicycle. Then it was me on my bicycle. The last one I remember, I wore a sailor uniform and my bicycle was covered in red, white and blue bunting. This was in the 40s, so most of the decorations were patriotic in theme.

I have a photograph of me one year on my decorated tricycle. In the photo, there is a bunch of Scouts standing behind me laughing, giggling and making fun of me and my one-person float. I look at that picture today and wonder what their reaction was when I was awarded the cash prize for first place in my division.

When I unearthed that photo many years later, Mother told me she thought the prize was $5. I know most of you folks in my age group remember that for a youngster, $5 was a small fortune in the 1940s. (That same photo graces the cover of this book.)

I think I won a prize (rather Mother really won but I got to keep the money) every year I was in the parade.

When I was older, I used to be amazed watching the May Day celebration in communist countries, especially Russia, where they held huge parades honoring the laborers and their great military might. Row after row of soldiers, truck-mounted missiles, tanks, cannons, and every kind of fighting machinery you can think of passing in review.

I watched these parades, remembering my May Day activities of years past, wondering what would be the reaction of the communist leaders, their lackeys and their suppressed subjects, if all of a sudden there was a break in the ranks of the military display, and along came a youngster in a white outfit, riding his tricycle decorated with bunting and flowers.

America proved to be a bastion of military might when it was called for, but back then we also retained our innocence, our compassion and our love of people and nation. May Day doesn't seem to mean much here any more, but every time it rolls around I get the desire to dress up and peddle through the community.

Chapter 4

World War II on Fraser Street

I was seven when the war started. I had a brand-new brother who was born in April, 1941, before the War started in December. We weren't rich by any means, but we got along. The house was filled with love, and by that standard, we were very wealthy.

Daddy was right at 40 so he wasn't drafted. He served on the home front, however. Being a member of the Rationing Board and a Civil Defense Air Raid Warden took a lot of his time. I think later on, he was appointed to the Draft Board.

We had to take extra precautions at our house to make sure all the light-proof shades were pulled and that we had on very few lights during the practice air raids. It would have made him look bad if his own house didn't meet the standards as he patrolled the streets.

It was probably more exciting than scary for a seven-year-old, but as I grew older and the war was still going on, I got more serious and worried about the conflict. I listened to the radio reports, and watched the news reels at the Saturday western movies with great intensity.

There were some frantic times as German submarines were reported off the South end of Pawleys Island, and at the mouth of Winyah Bay, 16 miles from downtown.

Every Family Was Touched

Later, I was closer to the war. I had four cousins who were involved in the fighting. My Mother's niece, Genny, came to live with us when her husband, Joe, was called into service. He became a half-track driver in an armored division.

Genny took over the bedroom that had belonged to my brother and me, but we didn't mind. We liked having her there. She was young and happy and could play any song on the piano that you could hum for her. She played by ear, and she was good.

Genny got a job at the rationing board that was less than a

block from our house. She used to read us Joe's letters about the service and being overseas. All of us gathered around the big, console Silvertone radio each night, hoping to hear some word about the outfits of some of the people we knew.

Every family tried to contribute to the war effort. I remember squeezing the very last drop out of the metal tooth paste tubes, then adding the empties to the box we kept on the back porch until it was full. Then we would turn it in for reprocessing.

We saved each tin can, mashed it flat and into the box it went. Aluminum was a big item for the war effort. Mostly what we gathered were old pots and pans. Tinfoil was another good item to contribute.

Exciting Times

I remember the great rush of adrenaline when an airplane flew over Georgetown. We'd grab our spotter books and eagerly flip pages to try to figure out first if it was an enemy plane. Deciding it wasn't an attacking craft, the next procedure was to try to discover the proper designation of the type "friendly" plane we had seen.

An occasional train would rumble into town carrying military hardware. Georgetown was the end of the line, so we didn't get any through traffic. But at Uncle Melvin and Aunt Lydie's house in Hemingway, it was a different story.

The train tracks there were right across the street, probably within 50 feet of their front porch. When we went there for a visit, I usually spent most of my time in a rocking chair waiting to see if a military train would pass by.

Lots of times I was lucky. The trains would slow down a bit going through the little town so you could get a good look. I remember one train had flat cars from the engine to the caboose loaded with Sherman tanks and half tracks. There must have been a hundred or more. I got to see transport trucks and jeeps and ambulances. Once the train had several navy airplanes, with their wings folded back as if they were stored on aircraft carriers.

Let's Play Soldier

All of us kids had some kind of play military uniform, a wooden rifle or pistol (no more metal toys during the war years), and other

16

"soldier" items. But Claude Kirkland and I had our own special war game we played.

We drew pictures of soldiers, airplanes, tanks, trucks and ships on notebook paper and then cut them out. I believe I spent a part of every day in school drawing my military arsenal. We had a standard size for each item. Each of us would then lay out our battlefield, and we would take turns attacking each other's forces.

The way we attacked was to stand over the elements with an old kitchen fork. We'd flip the fork, much like kids played mumble peg with a knife. Each time we "stuck" an opposing piece, it was ours. At the end of the game, the person who had "stuck" the most enemy pieces was the winner.

I had a great fork for a weapon. It was a real old, heavy, pewter-type one with five tines that came from my Grandmother's house. I got help sharpening the points so it would really stick. Sometimes if I hit the enemy piece sitting atop the root just right, I'd have to take two hands to pull the fork out.

Sometimes we played the game in my backyard under the pecan tree. But our favorite place to play was under the big oak tree that stood behind the auto parts store his father ran on Fraser Street. The trunk of that old tree had lots of roots running out from it, lots of indentions and ridges where you could place your battle elements. The store, Georgetown Auto Parts, was also a block from my house, right next door to the rationing board.

Better Equipped

When it came to playing war games among ourselves with other real people, I was a bit better off that some of the other kid soldiers. My cousins sent me all kind of military souvenirs from overseas. I had a real German bayonet, real parachute cords, real ammo pouches (the German ones were made of leather, US mostly out of canvas), hats and other parts of uniforms.

Herman, my cousin in the infantry, sent me a 410 gauge pistol, in a leather holster. He also sent home some Belgian made shotguns and rifles for my uncles. All of the rifles and shotguns came through the shipment, but evidently there was one censor who really took a liking to the 410 pistol that was supposed to be mine. He let the holster come through, but kept the pistol for himself. At least, that's what we figured.

I used to wear the holster with a piece of broom stick stuck in it for the weapon. Sometimes I'd wear a US helmet liner, sometimes a real German helmet. I had pistol belts, gas mask bags—a lot of stuff.

Why Not Have My Own Museum?

"You've got enough stuff to start a museum," Claude told me one day.

"Why not?" I agreed. "We could charge people to come see all my war souvenirs."

The garage in our backyard had a storage room on one end of it. There was nothing in it but mostly junk. The remainder of a plywood table I had tried to build to put my electric train on took up most of the room. I never used it much because I never could get it level enough so the track would stay together and the train would run straight.

We cleaned it out, propped up the table a bit, and started laying out the souvenirs. There was an old trunk in the room. We covered it with part of a parachute, and it made a great display area.

Finally, the museum was completed and we put a sign up on the sidewalk in front of the house. We thought about selling lemonade on the museum tours, but our folks didn't have enough sugar stamps left in their ration books. We drew a few visitors, probably not as many as we had hoped for, but the small amount of money we made was our fault.

We let our friends in for free, and that happened to be most of the kids at the school.

Our Family Was Lucky

Of all the relatives I was aware of in the war, every one of them came back. We were extremely lucky, and happy.

Keith Cribb, a cousin from Hemingway, was in the 8th Army Air Force. He was drafted after his freshman year at Clemson and entered the service in August, 1943.

Although trained as a waist gunner on a B-17 bomber, Keith flew seven missions as a "toggleer." Now I'll bet that's a term not even many of you World War II buffs will know.

"We weren't a lead bomber in our formation, and as a result didn't have a bombardier on board," he explained. "We didn't have one of the famous Norton Bomb Sights either. They gave me a quick course in releasing the bombs, and I operated a toggle switch which dropped them from the bomb bay.

"After those seven missions, we became a lead ship and got our bombardier and Norton Bomb Sight," he said, "and I went back to being a full-time waist gunner."

Keith flew 35 missions over Germany aboard the "Solid Sender," which carried the nose art of a fancy dude in a Zoot suit. On one mission, the plane was riddled with flack and machine gun fire and had to make a force landing in France. "We patched it up and limped on back to England," he said, "counting 87 holes in the fuselage when we finally made it home."

He recalls one mission when the formation was attacked by one of the new German jet fighter planes—the ME 262. "It was tremendously fast, but burned so much fuel it had a very limited range and time aloft. We were in a tight formation and he just made one pass and flew right on by us. We were happy to see him go."

Joe Lee, originally from Jefferson, was married to Mother's niece, Genny. Joe was finishing up his training at Ft. Knox. His unit was scheduled to be sent overseas when he got word that his Mother had died. He came home for the funeral, and while there, the unit shipped out. They eventually ended up in the Battle of the Bulge, but Joe, even though he was sent overseas later, never did catch up with the unit again.

William (Herman) Perry, also from Hemingway, was in the infantry, and he was in the Battle of the Bulge. At one stage of the fighting, he manned a quad .50 cal. anti-aircraft machine gun mounted on a halftrack. He came through without a scratch. Herman is Genny's brother.

In addition to being in the Army, he played a mean harmonica. He was a real hero of mine. Can you imagine when you weren't firing your quad .50 anti-aircraft machine gun, you could entertain yourself and your buddies by playing a couple of tunes on your mouth organ? Sounded like a real soldier to me.

Another cousin and the only one in the Pacific Theater was Ernest Cribb, Jr., from Georgetown. Ernest Junior proudly wore the uniform of a U.S. Marine. He, too, came home after the hostilities, however he brought a Purple Heart with him after being shot in the leg. Ernest Junior was a great baseball pitcher—a "lefty." We always hoped he would end up in the major leagues, but things didn't quite work out.

Lost Treasures

I have a few pieces of World War II memorabilia today, but not a single item that was in my childhood WWII museum. I don't know what happened to it, but somehow all those treasures got away from me.

Another thing I had was a collection of "Dimestore" Lead (or Toy) Soldiers. I used to buy one every time I got a few extra cents, mostly from McCrory's Dime Store on Front Street, about halfway between the Fire Station and Bodian's Department Store. The soldiers were displayed at the front end of the toy counter—each different pose occupying its own little partitioned square of the counter.

I liked the machine gunners best. Some of them were kneeling, some lying down. The anti-aircraft gunner and the bomb (grenade) thrower were great. I had the radio men with the tall antennas, the band pieces including the drummer, trumpet player, flag bearer and drum major. I guess I had more than a couple of shoe boxes full.

Don't have any of them left either. At today's prices, I guess my boyhood collection would have been worth several thousand dollars. But to me back then, they were toys to be played with, not collectibles to be saved until the market got right.

Another Loss

To me, the biggest loss we all face concerning the war years is the fact that very few people today remember the great patriotism that swept across this country from sea to sea. Young people (and I include everyone from Baby Boomers right on up those being born now) have no idea of the sacrifice, the loyalty, the unselfishness, the pride and the great ability that the men and women who fought for the literal freedom of the world exhibited in those years.

So many of them gave up their lives—the ultimate sacrifice—for the country so that those they left behind could continue to enjoy the great abundant life that only free people can experience.

I was 11 when the war ended, but I remember the great joy, the hugging, the dancing in the street, the prayers of thanksgiving. Hitler and Tojo had been defeated. Freedom lived, and so did we, thanks to those who gave so much.

I look at the meager mention in the history books school children "study" today about World War II and it makes me ashamed. I am ashamed that we're pretty soon going to let these great displays of courage and determination go unremembered—be forgotten.

Pretty soon, no one will remember. Most of the WWII veterans today are at least in their 70s. Those of us old enough at the time to actually remember some of what went on, are approaching that age. When we're gone, the only memories will be in books on shelves, on movie film and video tapes.

I hope somehow younger people can be encouraged to read, and watch, and remember, and honor those who gave so much.

Chapter 5

Dewey Altman—My Favorite Uncle

"How lucky I was to have an uncle like Dewey," I thought as I flipped the switch on the shiny dashboard one more time and then put my hands over my ears to shield them from the deafening scream of the siren.

Sitting high atop that bright red fire truck on the open driver's seat next to the Georgetown Fire Chief, I waved at people in cars and on the sidewalk and they all waved back. I knew they must envy me.

Dewey had to exercise the two fire trucks every now and then to make sure they'd run when the real fire call came in. Usually he'd leave the fire station on Front Street and head straight for my house. He'd pull up to the curb, sound the siren and I'd immediately drop what I was doing and climb aboard.

The station didn't have a dog mascot like you see so often, so Dewey always introduced me as his Dalmatian.

Notice I didn't call him Uncle Dewey. The title just didn't seem to fit, although he was always one of my favorite relatives. He was married to my Daddy's sister, so I didn't really feel obligated to call him uncle. I think he'd probably have corrected me if I had. He was Dewey—a free spirit, unlike most of the other uncles.

Dewey and Anna lived upstairs over the fire station right in the middle of downtown Georgetown. The Sampit River backed right up to the rear of the building. The wharf ran along the river, with a little cut-out space directly behind the station—like a great place to dock a fishing boat—a pretty good sized boat.

Anna worked a block away at Bodian's Department Store. Every time I went downtown, I had a refuge—either at the store, or at the fire station.

The Ever Popular Equipment Room

There was always a crowd around Dewey. He attracted the retired, those with a day off, those who didn't have a job—you name it, they were there. But on top of the regular crowd, he also attracted the rich and famous. When Tom Yawkey, owner of the Boston Red Sox, was in town at his plantation on South Island, often as not you'd find him at the fire station playing dominos with Dewey and the boys at a table set up in the equipment room.

In addition to housing all the fire-fighting gear that wasn't on the trucks, the equipment room with its flat-top coal heater also served as a great place to cook a fish stew, squirrel pilau (pronounced purr-low by locals), chicken bog or shrimp and crab boil. I believe those were the major delicacies.

When Bernard Baruch, famous Wall Street Baron and advisor to Presidents, was in town at his plantation Hobcaw Barony, a good part of the time you could find him on the bench in front of the fire station chatting with Dewey and the rest of the boys. Some said that once when President Franklin Roosevelt was visiting at Hobcaw Barony, Baruch brought him by the fire station in his limousine to introduce him to Dewey.

Dewey never would confirm this, but when asked about it, he'd just smile a big smile. "I'd better not talk about that right now," he'd say.

Sure Would Like to Have a Boat

One day while talking with Baruch about the outstanding run of big channel bass the charter boats were catching at the jetties which marked the mouth of Winyah Bay as it emptied into the Atlantic Ocean, Dewey mention that if he had a boat he could take out fishing parties on his time off and make a little money. Said he had an ideal place right there behind the station to keep the boat docked.

"I didn't know you wanted a boat," Baruch said. "Come to think of it, there's a 32-footer with a hole in the side of it half sunk near my dock. If you can raise it and patch the hole, you can have the boat."

"Thanks," Dewey said matter-of-factly. "I'll see about it."

Within a week, that boat was raised, pumped dry, the hole patched and towed to the "ideal place" behind the station. I was recruited to help clean it up and do a bit of remodeling. Dewey and I worked side by side.

23

Only problem was the engine. "I'm afraid it's shot," Dewey said. "You don't know anybody who might have an engine do you?" I didn't.

Couple of weeks later, Tom Yawkey came to play dominos. "Let me show you my boat," Dewey told him. They went on a tour. Dewey told him about Baruch giving him the boat. Also showed Yawkey the bad engine.

Not to be outdone by his friend, Yawkey rubbed his forehead. "Dewey, I'll declare I believe I've got a Chevrolet truck engine out at the place that'll fit that boat. If you'll go out there and get it, you can have it."

Next day when I went downtown after school, there was a wrecker backed up on the wharf as close to the boat as it could get. Dewey and a few of his friends were lowering that engine into the empty space where the shot one had been.

Suddenly, without any expenditure except for a few cleaning supplies and a few gallons of paint, it was Captain Altman, Charter Boat Skipper. Now there was another place for me to hide out for an hour or so when I went downtown.

Had Us A Charter Boat

During the summers, I was Dewey's mate up until the time I left to go to the University. The craft was right much of a tub. Kinda waddled forward at a top speed of six or seven knots. Took us a little more than two hours to make the 16 miles to the jetties, but it was paid for and the price had been right. "It's so wide, it's real stable in the water, even when the waves are running at a pretty good clip," Dewey described the boat.

"Slow but sure," he used to tell the customers. "Guarantee it'll get us there and get us back, even with the big load of fish we're going to catch."

And we really did. Often as not, members of the charter party would get seasick or drunk, or they'd get tired of fishing and want to play poker. But they wouldn't come back to the dock early. They had paid for that boat for the day and they were going to stay on it the whole time—sick or not.

While they threw up over the side, or drank or played poker, Dewey and I would catch fish. Of course they'd get the fish at the end of the day, but we had fun catching them. Once I hooked a giant ray with huge wings. It swam under the boat and attached itself to the bottom. Took us forever to get it loose. We finally had to crank up the boat and head in. Only then did it swim away.

Another time I hooked about a 30-40 pound channel bass and fought it almost up to the boat. One of the drunk fisherman demanded that I give him the rod and let him land the fish. Naturally I did—it was his money. Just as I put a gaff in the mouth of the fish to lift him aboard, a large shark swam by and severed the body of that bass just behind the head.

The drunk kept reeling and only stopped when the fish head hit the tip of the rod. He looked at the fish head and shook his own head. "Whoopee-Doggies, wonder how hard that thing would have fought if it had been a whole fish? You boys catch many just heads?"

I don't know how many years Dewey ran that charter boat. It was still fit when he died. I almost cried when Anna had to sell it to help her buy a house since she couldn't live in the fire house apartment any longer.

All of my aunts and uncles were great people, and I loved and enjoyed them. But Dewey was in a class by himself. Like they say, when God made Dewey, he retired the mold!

Chapter 6

Never Did Like Those Wimpy Toasters

In my opinion . . .

I start off with this statement because I realize that there are many more wimpy toasters in this country than there are non-wimpy toasters. This alone must indicate that my thinking is in the minority, yet I feel compelled to present my side of the story to you.

In my opinion, the purpose of a toaster is much more than to heat up a piece of bread and make it turn brown. There is a third purpose, and this is by far the most important.

The third purpose is to mash the hot, brown piece of bread flat!

Do you know the kind of toaster to which I'm referring? It looks something like a miniature pressing machine found in a laundry or dry cleaners. The top is not rigidly hinged at the rear, rather it floats to accommodate the thickness of the bread inside and will press even thick bread considerably flat. By adding the butter before the heating process, you end up with a melt-in-your-mouth delicacy.

Contrast this with the wimpy toaster that just accepts a piece of bread, drops it down a slot to be warmed and browned by heated coils of wire. When ready, the toast pops up, full width of the slice maintained with its bread integrity intact. Then you add the butter, almost as an afterthought.

Saturday Treat

The most vivid memory I have of my kind of toaster comes from early days when the Winyah Pharmacy was my immediate stop every Saturday afternoon after leaving the movie where I had just seen (probably several times) a cartoon, serial episode and western movie.

The next part of my Saturday treat was a toasted luncheon meat sandwich, bag of potato chips and a Coca-Cola. To this day I remember the delightful cuisine served up at the drug store. It consisted of mayonnaise, in unlimited quantity, spread on both pieces of bread; the better-than-average-size slice of luncheon meat, and the outside of both pieces of bread liberally brushed with melted butter.

This culinary masterpiece was then placed in a man-sized toaster, the top pressed firmly down, the heated metal plates in full contact with the bread.

What emerged was a FLAT sandwich—truly a feast fit for a young, western movie, famished fan. The heat, the mayonnaise, the melted butter did something to that slice of luncheon meat and bread which changed it into a sandwich connoisseur's dream meal. Sometimes, when finances allowed (meaning I sacrificed a drink or popcorn or candy bar during the movie) I had two sandwiches. This was truly the crowning glory of another memorable Saturday.

Probably the next best item to come out of such a toaster was a grilled cheese sandwich, especially when the cook scooped up the melted cheese that had run out from between the bread and ladled it on top.

I don't have a real toaster any more—haven't seen one for a long time. But then, I don't eat much toast now either. Even if I had a non-wimpy toaster, the luncheon meat or grilled cheese sandwiches, other than an occasional treat, wouldn't be allowed at this age—cholesterol, fat content, dairy products, etc. You know!

But I'd still like to have one of those toasters to introduce my grandchildren to a real piece of toast-hot, brown, pre-buttered, flat bread.

(P.S.—Shortly after this column was published, "Santee Cooper Country" and "Driftmaster Rod Holders" friend Calvin Baynard called and told me to drive down for a visit and pick up my "new but very used FLAT toast toaster." Seems he and Melva remembered one that had been stored in the back of one of their kitchen cabinets for years. They were willing to part with this treasurer. Well, I did visit, and I did pick up my toaster. It is no longer stored away, rather it is now used quite often. Not only do I occasionally enjoy FLAT sandwiches, I have also introduced my grandchildren to them, and every time I plug in that marvel, I revisit my childhood.)

Chapter 7

Front Porch Dreams

Sittin' and rockin' on the front porch was a great way to spend some time.

I did quite a bit of that during my formative years. You see, one of the most important and sacred areas of our home was the front porch. It is one of the great memories of my childhood. I spent many happy hours there, some with members of my family, some alone, just watching my tiny portion of the world go by.

The porch ran all the way across the front of our house and even wrapped around the corner on one end. The other end culminated in a one-car carport.

The end of the porch that wrapped around the corner was screened-in, and that's where most of family socializing took place from early spring 'till late fall. Daddy even had a desk out there so he could do most of his bookwork in the evening while Mother, my brother and I all gathered around to read and listen to the radio.

The rather large area was filled with rocking chairs. One was of cypress, made by my Grandfather who also was known for his cypress paddle boats. There were three others made of Wisteria vines with flat slats about one and a half inches wide for the back and seat. Mother had made tie-on cushions for each of the rockers. As a child, I remember thinking how unfortunate were people who had to sit in a chair that wouldn't move back and forth. Must have been so boring!

Another prominent furnishing of the screen porch was a metal glider with cushions. I took many an afternoon nap on that glider. It was a perfect place to read school books and do homework.

Watch the World Go By

One of the things that made our front porch so wonderful was the fact that it was located on Fraser Street. This also happened to be U.S. Highway 17, that ran between New York City and Miami,

Florida. Back then, before interstate highways, this was the main North-South route. We were at almost exactly the half-way point.

If television had been a reality in Georgetown back in the 1940s and early 1950s, it might not have been half as exciting or entertaining, but I could sit and rock, or glide, for hours and watch the world go by. It seemed that at least half of the cars that came by had out-of-state license plates.

In the winter, most of the traffic was headed South to Florida, in summer it reversed as the snow birds went back up North.

I remember I used to wonder how many of the cars that passed in front of my house contained celebrities—movie stars or band leaders or baseball players or famous singers. Surely there must have been some, but probably not half as many as I imagined.

If there wasn't a parade of fancy cars going by, there was local excitement like an occasional fire truck, police car or the daily delivery trucks or push carts of fruits and vegetables. There were ice cream vendors and ice trucks.

Great Sidewalks Too

All of the traffic wasn't on the highway. We had a great sidewalk that was always busy with people going to and fro. In the block North of my house was Poston's Grocery, a very popular emporium. Back then, housewives in town like my Mother, usually bought some groceries every day.

Poston's was a busy place. Buster, the butcher, was known to provide fine cuts of meat and he was always fair—never did weigh his thumb with the roast or the ham or chicken. Like most customers, we ran a tab there and paid off weekly or every other week.

In the block South of us was Georgetown Auto Parts, run by my best friend's father. There was also a popular radio repair shop and a building that housed the Rationing Board during the war, and later the town's only office supply store.

We knew most of the people who passed by on the sidewalk. There was a lot of stopping and visiting and waving. It was really exciting when a stranger walked by. That called for some quick investigation to see if any of the neighbors knew the "foreign" pedestrian.

Back Porch Was Almost as Good

Guess I'm giving most of the publicity to the front porch, but we also had a back porch that saw quite a bit of action. It was small—big enough for a table and four chairs, a cabinet and built-in closet. Both the cabinet and closet were the only "junk" areas of our house. You could find all kind of things in one or the other.

For my brother and me, the seasons of the year when we could eat at the table on the back porch were the best parts of the year. That table was probably only about 10 feet from the one in the kitchen, but because it was in a room partially open to the out-side—it was a different world.

Food served on the back porch had a much better taste that that served in the kitchen or the dining room. I distinctly remember how great iced tea was out there, and even milk was better. Ice cream was good anywhere, but we liked to churn it and eat it on the porch.

Lot of Growin'—Lot of Dreamin'

I did a lot of growing up on the front porch—did quite a bit of dreaming there too, perhaps even enjoyed a fantasy every now and then. It was a place where you could watch and be close to the world just across the 12-foot wide front lawn, but still be surrounded and protected by the security of home.

It was a place where you knew the different "feel" of each rocking chair. Even the front steps were special, a great place to sit and watch the "movie" of the highway.

From the time I left Georgetown to go to college, I've never lived in another house that had a front porch. I guess I miss that more than any other feature I recall about my childhood memories of home. It was so much better than TV.

For many years the front porch was an important factor in Ameri-can family life. It had a purpose, a personality. Today most houses have a front door and a "stoop" that only serves the purpose of giving politicians or other people you usually don't want to talk to, a place to lie in wait for you after they've rung the doorbell. Friends and family don't use the front door and "stoop."

My children grew up without the friendliness or the adventure or the security of a front porch, and they are poorer for the lack of it. Something drastic happened to that great institution. It went the way of the small touring circus that brought so much excitement to villages and towns; the great, black-smoke belching passenger and freight trains that once criss-crossed the nation and the wonderful voice adventure of the mind that was radio of yesterday. The era of the front porch also disappeared.

The young people of recent years seem to prefer a faster and more sophisticated way of life than we who first watched it in slow motion from front porches. To us it may seem a bit sad that this is so, for anything that speeds by unchecked is likely to go by unnoticed, until it reaches a point that makes necessary a gigantic correction to bring it back into being part of an acceptable way of life. Perhaps one day they'll come to the realization that not all things of the past were automatically bad.

I hope you had a front porch. They aren't so popular today. About the only people who have one are people who have bought old homes and remodeled them.

Back porches are in about the same category, but lots of people do have decks or patios that kinda take the place of the "heaven in the rear." Even today, when I walk outside from early spring 'till late fall, I can close my eyes and remember the joy in my heart and in my taste buds when I arrived home to find the table on the back porch set for a meal.

And then, after the dishes were cleaned and put away, it was back to the front porch to relax, talk, listen to the radio and watch the world go by.

I remember everything being much more simple and uncomplicated back then. Maybe it was because I was young—didn't have a lot of responsibilities. If I only had a front porch and a back porch today, I could probably determine whether or not things are more complicated, or if it's just because I'm older with lots of responsibilities.

I guess I'll never know, but it's fun to ponder.

I'm thinking maybe it would do all of us some good if we could return to that front porch mentality and be able to once again view the world from a place of friendliness and security.

Chapter 8

"I'm a Real Reporter/Photographer"

I walked into *THE GEORGETOWN TIMES* shortly after I turned 14 and made that announcement to the Editor.

It was early January after I'd gotten my Argus C-3, 35mm camera for Christmas. It was by far the best camera I'd ever owned. True, I'd been playing around with photography and had my own very primitive darkroom in the Mozley's attic for a year or two. They lived next door to us. They didn't use their attic, so I asked if I could.

But I had been taking pictures with little fix-focus cameras that used 127 sized film. The Argus was a real camera! It was a 35mm rangefinder model that focused when you turned the wheel and you could read on a scale what the distance was from the camera to the subject. It had a flash unit and a light meter to help you figure out what the exposure setting should be. Only thing I had to do now was figure out how to use it.

"I've been working on the Winyah High School *Student Prints Newspaper* sports section," I told the *TIMES* Editor, "I know how to type and I can take photographs with my new camera and develop them myself. I'll make you a good reporter."

"Yes, we need somebody to cover high school football and maybe do a few feature stories," he told me. I grew taller with each word he spoke.

How Do You Load This Thing?

I left the newspaper and went to my friend, the pharmacist, at Walgreens. "You know a lot about cameras don't you?" I asked.

"A little bit," he said, kneeling down to get on my level. He was tall and kind and always willing to help out. He'd sold me an Underwood portable typewriter last year and let me pay on the installment plan. That was long before lay-away in the Georgetown retail business community.

I was still paying—hadn't missed one yet. Pretty soon it'd be mine and I could take it home. You see, he sold me the typewriter on the installment plan, but because I was underage and couldn't enter into a contract, I didn't get the typewriter until I'd paid the entire amount. He didn't charge me interest though and that was a big help.

"Let's take a look at this camera. What did you want to know?"

"First of all, could you show me how to put the film in it? Then maybe you'd help me figure out how to read this light meter."

I was a real, professional photographer all right.

Years later, after I'd been making my living, or at least a part of it on photography for a long time, I looked back on that experience and wondered whether or not it was a good move. Yeap, I finally decided. I think it was.

I sold a picture to the newspaper off that first roll of film that the pharmacist loaded for me, and I was hooked. Photography was it. Photography and reporting. I learned a new term that January— photojournalism.

Professor Robert Edwards

The first story I did for *THE GEORGETOWN TIMES*, and that first picture I sold them, was about our high school chemistry teacher— Mr. Edwards.

He was quite the catch for Winyah High. He moved south after retiring from one of the Ivy League Colleges, I believe it was Colgate. He was a full professor. Wanted to get away from the cold up north, the big city hustle and bustle, and all that.

He bought a home in the deep woods around McClellanville and came to teach at Winyah. He loved teaching as much as he loved the primitive life he chose for his retirement. As it turned out, all of us at Winyah were the better because of him.

He was "it" as far as we were concerned. At first, we were in awe of this Yankee college professor. But it didn't take us long to number him among our favorites. He didn't worry about the little things that other high school teachers worried about. After all, he was used to college-aged kids and he treated us the same way he had treated them.

We could chew gum in class! We could get up and walk around the room. Question him when he made a statement. He loved it when we didn't take everything he said for granted.

He did the teaching, but he left the learning up to us. Knowledge was there in abundance if we wanted it, but we had to supply the initiative. Once we did, he really cut loose and taught us chemistry by the truck load.

He respected us if we deserved it, put up with us if we didn't. When we did well, he was happy for us. When we dropped the ball, he let us know he was there to help us if we wanted him to.

He invited us to his home and showed us his collection of insects, butterflies, artifacts he'd dug around the area. He didn't treat us like guest or students or nuisances. He treated us like friends.

I guess some of us kinda tried to test him at the beginning. Some felt it necessary to let him know that he wasn't so smart because he was from up North, and we weren't so dumb because we were from the South.

Funny thing is, thoughts like that never entered his mind. From the first, he didn't put up with any foolishness or disrespect. He let us know that respect was a two-way street. He expected to earn our trust, and we had to earn his. It was a very short period of time before he didn't have to worry about foolishness or lack of respect any more.

He liked the article I did about him. The newspaper liked the article. I liked it too, and I was on my way.

Sports Correspondent

I covered all school sports for the TIMES. I decided that if I could walk in off the street and get a job as a reporter/photographer, then maybe I could do the same thing with a phone call.

After talking with the sports department at several daily newspapers, I ended up being their Georgetown STRINGER (an "in" term for correspondent and one that I liberally sprayed around the neighborhood at every opportunity).

I was working for *THE STATE* in Columbia, *THE MORNING NEWS* in Florence, *THE NEWS AND COURIER* and *THE CHARLESTON EVENING POST* in Charleston. A year later, *THE CHARLOTTE OBSERVER* came on board.

I was paid by so much per inch of copy that was published, extra for photos. I started a college fund with part of the money, spent the rest on kid things, like gas and hot dogs and shotgun shells and .22 rifle bullets.

Better Than the First Job

My first job, other than helping out on my uncle's farm in the summer handing tobacco and driving the crates, turned out to be both a disaster and a blessing.

Just down the street from us, about a block and a half away, was the local feed and seed farm store. They had a plant that processed chickens for the market. I'd been looking for a job for a while without any success when they agreed to try me out.

I showed up bright and early the first morning, wearing my knee-high rubber boots and something over my head as they had instructed. Didn't know why, but it wasn't long before I found out.

They showed me how to run the "plucking machine" which scrubbed the feathers off the chickens. It was a big, round drum with lengths of rubber garden hose sticking out in all directions.

From that, they taught me the art of cutting up a fryer. To this day, I'm still pretty good at that. I spent the rest of the morning wielding that knife.

The aroma of a chicken processing plant isn't what you'd call one of your favorites, no matter who you are. I made it through the morning, went home for lunch where I first peeled off the boots and the hair covering. It had completely changed color. Better it than my hair, I thought. The boots were as wet inside as they were outside.

After lunch, I returned to the line and started cutting up those fryers that were coming through. I did notice that they were some-what bigger than the ones on the morning run, but it really didn't make much of an impression on me.

That is until a couple hours later when the foreman came up to my position. He was right mad I guess. His face was red, he was breathing hard—actually kinda snorting. "Cribb," he hollered, "why are you cutting up those hens? We don't cut up hens. People cook hens whole, they fry fryers by the piece—that's why we cut up fryers. We don't cut up hens. You've probably ruined half the run of hens in part of one afternoon."

I handed him the knife, my head covering and trudged across

the sloppy, wet floor and out the door. That was the end of my chicken processing career. I'll say this for him though, he did pay me for a whole day. Mailed me the check. It didn't have a note or anything in the envelop, just the check.

I decided right there that my next job would be something a little more fun to do, wouldn't smell and wouldn't require that my feet be sloshing around in wet chicken entrails inside my boots all day. My next job was with *THE GEORGETOWN TIMES*!

Lucky Me

I was one of the lucky youngsters. None of this, "I'm going to college but I don't know what I want to be."

I knew from age 14 that I was going to the University of South Carolina and major in Journalism. Writing was my love then, and it has lasted now for more than half a century.

It was much better than working with chickens. I think it was a pretty good decision. I hope you think so too.

Chapter 9

Who Turned the Radio on?

I think the radio must have been playing when Dr. Bruorton delivered me that morning in late November, 1934, at our house on King Street in Georgetown. Perhaps when you hear the world's sounds unrestrained for the first time, you like what you heard and remember it.

The radio has been "on" most of my life. It has played a big part in my existence, and even today, I prefer it to TV. When I'm in the car, I'm listening to radio. There are nine of them in our house, so whether I'm in the storage room outside, cooking in the kitchen, even in the bathroom—you guessed it.

My Ambition—WGTN

Even though I was writing for *THE GEORGETOWN TIMES* and several other newspapers while in high school, my real ambition was to be on the radio. I wanted to be a disc jockey, read the news and anything else that came along.

Our local station was WGTN, a full 250 watts! It didn't rival the "power stations" of the nation like WSM and KDKA, WSB, KMOX and others, but it did its job in keeping Georgetown citizens informed and entertained—you could almost pick it up all the way to Pawleys Island! Well, most of the time.

Affiliated with the Mutual Broadcasting System, it was owned by two community spirited people—Joe and Mamie Delzell, they always had room on the staff for at least one high school student. At the time I started my campaign for the job, staffer Reed Swan was a senior in high school and I knew he'd be leaving for college the next year. Reed had been hired when Eddie Skinner, another Winyah student, graduated and moved on.

I practically lived at the station after school. I thought the more I was around, the more Joe and Mamie would see that I was really interested and really wanted the job. I guess I tried any course of action to let them know how much I wanted to work for them.

I hung around, in addition to begging them 10 or 15 times a day to hire me.

They finally gave me a tryout, probably as much to get me off their backs as anything else. I passed!

Back then, on a station like WGTN, when you were on the air—you were it. During the week, Mamie worked up front handling all the advertising accounts. Joe was out selling advertising, and whoever was on the air was announcer, newscaster, engineer, producer and whatever else came up.

They did start me out writing advertising copy and news copy for a few weeks before I did much on-air stuff, but once they put me on the air, I was expected to handle everything that came along.

Youngest in the Country

After I'd been at the station for only a couple of months, Mamie did me a real favor. One of the Mutual Network programs we carried every weekday night was "Eugenie Baird's On and Off the Record." She was a middle-aged band singer who really reached her career high with Glen Gray and the Castle Loma Orchestra.

Mutual set her up with her own radio show from New York City. She'd bring in a disc jockey from some station on the network in various parts of the country for a week. They'd discuss the top songs in the visitor's area of the country, and use them on the program. Eugenie would perform live (she had a small combo in the studio), and on the top hits she played the records by the artist who had the best version of the song.

Mamie wrote Eugenie and told her she should invite me since I was the youngest disc jockey at any station on the Mutual network. Sure enough the invitation came right back. Two weeks before Christmas in 1952, I boarded a train and headed for New York. It was the first trip I'd every made alone. I was 17.

Mother and Daddy bought me a new suitcase, an overcoat and a real man's felt hat because they said it would be cold in New York. They took me to Kingstree early Sunday morning to catch the train. I wore that hat until I got inside the train car. Then I packed it away until the train was approaching the Kingstree station on the way home after my week in the big city. I got it out and put it back on before I got off to greet my parents.

When I arrived at Grand Central Station, there was no one there to meet me. I had a copy of my hotel reservation and an address for the hotel. The Eugenie Baird show wasn't used to dealing with under-age announcers.

Boy, did I feel important. A bit scared, but important. I hailed a Red Cap, told him my plight, and I was in good hands. He was originally from South Carolina, so he took care of me. Put me in a cab and instructed the driver: "No tricks. Take this young man to this address, he's going to pay you $1.75 for the ride and not a penny more. Understand me?"

I checked in at the hotel and then realized I had time on my hands until 5:30 Monday afternoon. That's when I had to report to Mutual headquarters for the show.

I was, in fact, on my own for the entire week. I'd show up at the studio, rehearse, do the show and I was free as a bird in New York City until the next night. The crew did take me out to supper one night. We went to a basement restaurant that was dimly lit, and Italian, and had secluded tables in the back. That's where we sat. I couldn't help thinking it must have been a "Speakeasy" back during prohibition. I don't know whether or not I enjoyed my meal— I was too busy waiting for the Mafia to come in.

Big Wheel

The show's producers did arrange some tours for me. I did the usual tourist things like Rockefeller Plaza and the Christmas Show, the Statue of Liberty, Empire State Building and the like.

I guess the biggest thrill was a visit to Arthur Godfrey's TV show where I got to sit on the stage very close to the man himself. He introduced me as a visiting dignitary to New York and the Mutual Broadcasting System.

I got telegrams from the Mayor, Winyah High School Principal, School District Superintendent and lots of family and friends. Eugenie read them on the air, and a lot of the scripts for the week were centered around what I did back home in Georgetown, and the town itself.

Living High

You might think it would have been a letdown to come back to Georgetown and 250-Watt WGTN after broadcasting to the entire nation for a week, but it wasn't. Just so long as they poked a microphone in front of my face, I felt at home and important.

As I mentioned before, when you work at a small station, you really learn a lot about the business, and quickly. I was host for every kind of music program we did—country, rhythm and blues (as it was known back then), popular, religious.

Ah, religious! That was an experience in itself. One of the top revenue producers for WGTN and stations of its type was the Sunday morning parade of preachers and gospel groups who pay for 15 or 30 minutes of air time (whatever the collections they'd received from the previous week allowed them to buy), and then proceed to do their preaching and singing and praying, even funeral announcements.

Mind you, I'm not making fun of them, but it was quite an experience for a 17-year-old. Joe and Mamie instructed us to keep the door locked on Sunday morning, therefore everyone who came to buy time and to perform had to wait on the sidewalk in front of the station.

We'd go to the front door, crack it slightly and call out the name of the next group that was supposed to go on. If they weren't there, we'd call out the name of the next group, and so on down the line. When we ran out of names of people who had scheduled time, there were always a few groups who had shown up in hopes of getting to go on if somebody else failed to come.

Once a group was permitted into the studio, they could do anything they wanted for how many minutes they'd bought. There was some wild preaching and praying and singing that went on. Sometimes they'd bring more musicians than we had room for in the big studio. In that case, we'd put the overflow out in the hall and rig up another microphone out there for them.

Swingin' and Swayin' and Prayin'

It was not unusual for me to be sleepy on early Sunday mornings. Once I had a preacher show up without an accompanying chorus or group of people. This was unusual because it seemed

40

that one way to judge the success of a program was by the number of other people in the studio who could pronounce an "Amen" after the speaker made a point.

Anyway, this lone preacher began his sermon over the airways. In the studio, we had a microphone that hung from the ceiling on a rope and pulley. Some performers preferred to stand, others to be seated. We could raise or lower the mike as needed.

This preacher wanted to stand, so I adjusted the height, closed the door and went into the control room. It was separated from the studio by a large glass window. I took my seat and proceeded to nod a bit as the preacher cranked up. This wasn't unusual, I often relaxed while the different groups were on the air.

But this morning, I went completely to sleep. The preacher had paid for 15 minutes. All I remember is being suddenly awaken by a tremendous "Wham . . . Thump" in my headphones. I jerked upright in my seat and turned to the window. The poor preacher had evidently swung his arms wildly during the sermon, hit the microphone and it was swinging from side to side.

He was swaying wildly back and forth, bible in one hand, damp handkerchief from wiping his brow, in the other, trying to keep in front of the mike as it was swinging. At the same time, he was trying to get my attention, moving the hand with the handkerchief across his throat motioning to me to "CUT."

Evidently he had run out of prepared material and was very frustrated because I had let him run on beyond his paid-for time—at least 30 minutes beyond.

Oh well, it worked out OK. Joe usually listened to the station every minute and anytime we made a mistake, the phone would be ringing. But for some reason he wasn't listening that morning. I was just glad the preacher "thumped" that microphone, or no telling how long I would have let him preach.

A Few Mistakes

I did manage to make a few mistakes, and I got my quota of phone calls from Joe. One of my favorite duties was the morning and late afternoon news sponsored by that petroleum giant—ESSO. I did a 10-minute news program twice a day billed as the ESSO reporter (for you youngsters, what was ESSO then is EXXON now).

I though it was a bit ironic because I never used ESSO gasoline—our family had always bought Gulf gasoline just three doors from our house from Mr. Tiller, and later from Vonnie Carraway who had always worked there and then took over ownership himself.

On the early morning show, I guess my mind was wondering a bit when I announced to the world: "Drive into your ESSO station and fill up with that Good Gulf gasoline!"

RING . . . RING . . . RING. Guess who that was on the telephone. I had already corrected myself on the air, but the damage had been done. Fortunately none of the local ESSO family was listening that morning. But Joe was!

On to College

I really hated to graduate from Winyah High. I was looking forward to going to USC in Columbia and getting my formal education in Journalism, but I really hated to leave the radio station and the newspapers. I was doing pretty good, had a fair college fund in the bank, but like the teacher said, if I wanted to be a Journalist, I really needed to study how to do it.

I nodded in agreement, but secretly wondered what they thought I had been doing these last few years. My radio career was to the point where Joe and Mamie hated to see me leave, and none of the newspapers had complained about my writing.

Fortunately, at least for me, it didn't end there. I joined the staff of the University's student station, WUSC Radio. It was a very low wattage station designed to cover most of the campus in Columbia. This was lots of fun, but no pay. I didn't last long there because I needed the extra money to help pay my expenses.

WNOK-TV was where I landed next. I thought TV might be a lot like radio, but it wasn't. I worked on the floor crew instead of the announcer's booth. That meant I helped build sets, put up lighting and ran a camera for programs that originated from the studio.

I left TV when I got a job as Legislative Correspondent for *THE FLORENCE MORNING NEWS*. Since Joyce was from Florence, that worked out just fine. I worked at the paper during one summer vacation. Then I met Paul Benson who had Radio Station WJMX in Florence. It was the home station for the Darlington Raceway

Network. Working for the station during the summer led to my becoming a member of the broadcast team for the NASCAR races held in Darlington for the rest of the time I was in college.

Talk about flying high! I got to hobnob with the drivers and car owners and track officials. For weeks before a race, we spent all our free time at the raceway getting to know the layout and idiosyncrasies of the track, the pit crews and the drivers.

My position on the broadcast team was midway between turns three and four. They parked the station's panel truck there and I used it as a platform so I could see the cars coming down the back straightaway, through turns three and four, and into the front straightaway.

Once a wheel came off one of the cars in a wreck and was bouncing my way. I laid down on top of the truck because I was afraid it might hit the side and rock the vehicle, causing me to lose my balance. Laying down was the best thing I ever did. That wheel hit a rut or rock or something and bounded completely over the top of the truck—right where I'd been standing. I was so shook up I could hardly talk, but the team said that was the best race description I'd ever given!

That was in the days of people like Joe Weatherly, Curtis Turner, Fireball Roberts, Buck Baker, Tiny Lund and Fred Lorensen (he was a young hotshot of that time). Junior Johnson, Cale Yarborough, Richard Petty—they were making names for themselves.

Racing was exciting, but then so was everything involved with radio as far as I was concerned. Although I didn't follow up my career in it after college, I never lost my love for broadcasting.

I Owe Them

Radio has opened lots of doors for me, given me some excitement and generally helped my career.

I've met lots of good people who encouraged me along the way as I did learn to be a photojournalist, photographer, writer and communicator in general, but few have had my true interest at heart and maintained a genuine concern in my career as did Joe and Mamie Delzell.

One more addition I'd have to make to that list are Jack and Mary McGrail. Jack was my photography instructor at USC, and hired me to be his student assistant in the photo lab. I can say, without a doubt, he was the most knowledgeable and educated person I've ever known, and he didn't have a college degree. In addition to teaching, he was *THE STATE* Newspaper's Chief Photographer for many years.

His wife, Mary, was a talented photo retoucher and colorists and artist. She provided the "color" in color portraits before color film became common and popular. They didn't have children, but were almost like "Columbia parents" to Joyce and me. Mary even taught Joyce a bit about coloring photos.

When I wrote my book on freelance photography, I dedicated the book to: "My family, and to Jack and Mary McGrail, who shared their knowledge and their friendship." I've never written anything more accurate or meaningful to me than that statement.

Chapter 10

Pawleys Island

It was my second home.

A quiet, serene setting, with a wide, white, almost always secluded beach where you could do family things and not have to worry about your space being crowded, or your enjoyment being interrupted. That was Pawleys Island. Cottages, and sand, and dunes, and blue sky, and blue waters, and fishing and crabbing were the principal ingredients of a visit there.

People who love Pawleys have always striven to keep the island free of commercial establishments, relegating them to the U.S. Highway 17 area that bounded it on the west side. In my childhood, I remember one small grocery store on the island, but it didn't last too long. The building was eventually turned into an apartment complex.

There was a bowling alley run by the King family, I believe. They also had a small snack bar, beach and chair rentals and a snow cone cart. The only other commercial venture I remember was a small real estate office.

Of course, there was the pavilion. Nobody considered it a business though. It was part of the island experience—a way of life, an institution. More on it later.

There was a hue and cry when an outfit built condominiums in the area where the popular fishing pier was. What hurt us more than anything else was that the fishing pier went from a public facility to a private one.

Two Weeks of Paradise

We always took our two weeks vacation at Pawleys, even before we owned a cottage there. For many years, we rented one of the ground level apartments at Mrs. Rucker's huge house.

The apartment was good sized. Uncle Frank, Aunt Louise and their daughter Sarah went with us every year, as did Anna (another aunt). Uncle Frank, Daddy and I (and my brother Alan after he

45

came along) spent part of every day fishing off the strand. We'd catch Whiting, Spots, Croaker and an occasional Puppy Drum or Flounder on our big salt water rods and reels. We used a variety of bait including cut shrimp, sand fleas, fiddler crabs and cut bait (strips cut off a small fish.)

Frank used to get a bit irritated because he thought I wasn't paying attention to my fishing. One afternoon when I was about 11 or 12, I grew a bit tired and sat on top of the bucket full of tackle we always took along. I was drawing pictures in the sand with the tip of my rod.

"Look at him," he said to Daddy, "sitting there instead of standing up. If he got a bite he wouldn't know what to do with it."

About that time, I did get a bite. Pulled in the biggest Puppy Drum (Spot Tail Bass or Red Fish) not only of the week but the largest fish we'd caught in the last year or two. Frank didn't say anything more about me not paying attention.

Pulling the Seine

Uncle Fred, Mother's brother from Hemingway, would usually come down for a day and bring one of his big seine nets. He was a commercial fisherman—caught Shad and Sturgeon and Catfish (back then it was legal to net Sturgeon and to use the seine.)

Several of us smaller family members would stay on the beach and anchor the wooden pole attached to one end of the net, while the bigger, stronger ones would wade out into the ocean pulling the other pole and make a big semi-circular sweep, ending up on the land a hundred or so feet away.

That provided a real seafood smorgasbord—bounty from the sea. The net would usually be loaded with crabs, all the kinds of the same type fish we usually caught on rod and reel, and occasionally a few shellfish. Then there would be other less desirable creatures like Jellyfish, Stingrays, Starfish and maybe a small shark or two.

Some of the youngsters didn't want to go swimming in the ocean after they saw what we pulled in with that net, but that fear usually wore off in an hour or two.

Everybody within sight on the beach would gather around with "ohs and ahs" when they saw the operation going on. That made us youngsters feel important as we explained to the uninitiated what we were doing and what we were catching.

Our Own Cottage

After the war, Daddy had been able to buy a small lot on the North end of the Island, but we couldn't afford to build a house on it. We considered ourselves lucky when a neighbor wanted that lot so he could enlarge his house, and offered to trade us a piece of land on the South end of the Island that had a structure on it.

I said structure instead of a house because that's a better description. The building had been the old Coast Guard Station used for beach patrol headquarters during World War II. It was on the extreme Southern tip of the island, probably a couple of miles from the lot. The man who owned the lot bought that prefabricated building and had it moved up to this location.

Daddy didn't think twice about trading. The building needed some work, but it had already been placed on stilts about three feet off the ground and was in fair condition. I remember going inside for the first time. The floor was covered with sand, up to a couple of feet deep in the corners. There were giant cans of food throughout the house, like gallon cans of peaches and pears and different kinds of vegetables.

I searched for any military treasures that might have been left behind, but canned food was all I ever found.

Lots of family members pitched in to get the place in shape. Uncle Jimmy was a plumber and also did some electrical work. He handled that for us, and everybody did carpentry work, painting, etc. We hand-made the doors for the three bedrooms and bathroom, even made a table that would seat 10 people, 12 in a pinch.

The center of the interior was a tremendous room that served as a living room, den, dining room, playroom and even had a couple of daybeds in it which could be used to sleep visitors. There were four areas opening from this big room—two on either side. These made three bedrooms and a kitchen. Between one bedroom and the kitchen was a hall leading to the bathroom and a side, screened-in porch. There was also a porch on the front of the house and on the back.

The front porch was filled to capacity with rocking chairs. These

47

rockers probably saw more use than anything else in the house.

No Thanks to Hugo

We enjoyed that little house, which Mother named The Cozy Crib, from the late 40s until Hurricane Hugo took it from us in 1989. We had our two weeks every summer and then rented it out the rest of those warm months. Every time there was a vacant week, which wasn't often, we would head back over to Pawleys for a bonus vacation.

In the winter, we would usually go over for several weekends. The big "Bull Whiting" and the tasty Spots were abundant in the surf in late September and October. Several years, when housing was in short supply in Georgetown, we rented the house for the entire winter. I always felt a bit "cheated" to know we couldn't go in our own house for that long a time, but the extra money sure came in handy. Daddy said a beach house takes lots of upkeep. Thank goodness we didn't have to worry about things like that, and it was nice to see him not have to worry either.

Great Place to Shag

The old Pawleys Pavilion was the only night spot around. Always crowded with teenagers and older young people, we considered it the home of the Shag, about half way between a slow dance and the jitterbug.

I'll never forget the thrill when I was old enough to go to the Pavilion. In all, there have been three of them. The one most prominent in my memory was the second pavilion on the island. It was built on stilts over the marsh near the Northern causeway. In fact, all three of them were built out over the marsh.

I remember when it burned down in 1957. Lots of young beach goers were devastated. A few years later, some prominent citizens got the ball rolling and built a new one. It also burned, but the powers that be decided not to try again. Pawleys has been pavilionless since 1966.

Don't know how we would have grown up without it. Don't know how the young people of today are able to grow up without it. The Pavilion is gone, but the spirit remains and memories of good times remain.

Grandchildren Grew to Love Pawleys

After Alan and I both had families, our children were able to experience Pawleys as they were growing up. This was a wonderful house for children. It was high enough off the ground so they could play in the sand under it. There was an outside shower so they could wash off after swimming or sanding.

And if they did come in with wet suits or sandy feet and bottoms, nobody got upset. The furniture was either old or had plastic covers which would dry or brush off easily. Sand on the linoleum floor was easily swept outside.

With three porches, they could always get away from each other and find their own space when they needed to. It was about equal distance from the ocean, or the creek which was the back boundary of the island, so we could always take our choice of swimming hole.

Although we enjoyed the quite, easy life on Pawleys, it was nice a couple of nights to go to wild, noisy, exciting, crowded Myrtle Beach. The rides and games were fun for the kids, and bearable for the adults, knowing pretty soon we'd be back to peace and quiet.

Going out to eat seafood at Murrell's Inlet, the seafood capital of the world, was worth the trip also. I've eaten seafood on three continents, including much of this country, Mexico and Canada, but I've never found any finer.

Chefs at the Inlet have told me that the real secret is fresh-from-the-sea catches, and fresh oil in which it is deep fried. They know the precise moment to remove the food from the fryer, so it is done, but not overcooked—juicy but not mushy. Another secret is to serve the food as soon as it is taken off the fire. Most good restaurants probably have as many people preparing the individual plates as they do cooking the food.

Pawleys Island is probably about as close to paradise as I ever expect to get on this earth. I really can't think of a better place to spend a vacation, and for some people, to spend a life. Our children grew to feel it was their second home also. But all of that changed with Hugo.

Chapter 11

Red Rice 'N Duck

When I was growing up in Georgetown, Saturday was always a special day of the week. In the morning or afternoon, or morning and afternoon, it was a western movie, followed by our entire family eating out that night at the Gladstone Hotel.

The Gladstone no longer occupies its spot on Front Street (Georgetown's main street), having been torn down in 1971 after 131 glorious years standing guard over the bustling activities of this quaint seaport town.

Gone is the building, but not the wonderful thoughts of those Saturday night meals—I guess you could call them a "Saturday Night Special!" You see, the Gladstone was famous for a dish which I doubt is served by any other restaurant anywhere—red rice and duck. There were other specialties too like shad dinners and golden, yellow cornbread. This delicacy was enjoyed with slabs of melting butter and glasses of cold buttermilk. Mind you, the dining wasn't limited to Saturday nights, but for our family Saturday and Gladstone were synonymous.

But the red rice and duck are what I recall with fondest memories. They come closer to "gourmet eating" than any other dish to which I've been exposed.

Chef Tony Parker

Tony Parker, a round, happy, full-of-fun man, was one of the genius chefs who prepared this treat. Oliver Robinson was another. The roast duck was tender and flavorful, while the red rice was doctored with ample hot sauce so as to really tingle the taste buds— while being on the verge of prohibitively hot.

My parents tell me that many a time they saw tears come to my eyes as I continued to shovel in that spiced-up rice, soothing the fire in my mouth with fresh milk and cornbread.

The expansive dining room of the Gladstone, just a touch below sidewalk level, was dotted but not crowded with square tables covered with the whitest table cloths you've ever seen. Each chair also had a sparkling white back cover. Waitresses wore white uniforms and friendly smiles that never faded.

The Gladstone's history is practically nonexistent in written form. This is unusual since, for so many years, it housed travelers and provided its famed menu for so many people who journeyed to Georgetown for the sole reason of dining there.

Julian Bolick, the late author of articles and books related to Georgetown places and people, touched briefly on the Gladstone in his book *GEORGETOWN HOUSELORE*. In it he said: " . . . One of the last of the old Front Street Houses, this stands out in front of buildings more modern in design.

"After the Civil War, Mrs. Logan, a lady who lost her fortune during the conflict, lived there. She was a quaint little lady, taking in roomers and selling milk and butter for a livelihood. She had great pride in the quality of her products and those who were permitted to purchase them considered it quite an honor.

"After her death, the place was purchased by Mr. S. M. Gladstone who operated it as a hotel. His widow continued there and made it famous for shad and red rice and duck dinners."

The Gladstone was a landmark which served travelers to Georgetown of yesteryear. Many visitors from the uplands and all of South and North Carolina, and occasionally from a more distant state, have passed beneath the wide piazza that sat, without apologies, astride the sidewalk fronting Georgetown's busy main street.

Its visitors entered the warm hospitality of the friendly dining room to enjoy foods which were said to be the best the Lowcountry had to offer. Mr. and Mrs. Gladstone welcomed everyone who came to the hotel as if they were a long-time friend. Often they would sit with diners as they enjoyed their meal, and would call for special dishes to be sent to the table or special services for their guests.

After her husband's death, Mrs. Gladstone presided over the hotel and dining room, following the friendly tradition which impressed visitors as much as the fantastic menu.

It is truly unfortunate that Chef Parker's recipes for red rice and duck were evidently never written down, but through research with those who remember the great taste, and with others who have their own recipes for the red rice, we've come up with a combination which those involved believe is about as close as we can come to the original.

It is printed here for you to try if you'd like. Keep in mind that you can make it as hot or as mild as you wish by the amount of hot sauce and pepper you choose to use.

I hope some of you who read this will be among the truly fortunate who can recall dining at the Gladstone in old Georgetown. If so, I'm sure you'll share my fond memories from childhood of a place that was in itself memorable, and of people who truly cared about their visitors and guests.

The Gladstone is gone, but it will never be forgotten by those who enjoyed its hospitality, its friendliness and its unforgettable red rice and duck.

(With appreciation to Margaret Ann Tarbox for allowing the use of material from Julian Bolick's "Georgetown Houselore.")

Georgetown Red Rice

1/4 lb. bacon*
1/2 cup chopped onion
2 cups rice
2 1/2 cups red tomatoes
1 cup broth (duck, chicken, turkey)
1/3 cup catchup (or catsup or ketchup)
1/2 tsp. salt
1/4 tsp. pepper
1/8 tsp. hot sauce (amount optional)

Cook bacon, remove from pan and crumble. Cook onions in bacon fat until tender, then add rice, tomatoes, broth, catsup, seasonings and crumbled bacon. Cook on low heat until rice is done, stirring several times during cooking.

*Fatback may be used instead of bacon. Fry out fatback but remove before it gets hard. Dice fatback and add to rice.

Chapter 12

Golf Team Substitute

To give you an idea of the degree of my skill in this athletic endeavor, which originated in ancient Scotland and should have stayed there, I spent my high school career as a bench warmer on the golf team. Yes, I was a substitute. That is except for one brief moment of semi-glory.

My short-lived tenure as a Winyah High School Golf Team starter began early one Friday morning. The team was set for a match on the Municipal Course in Charleston at one o'clock with one of the local schools.

One of our regular team members came up sick and couldn't make the trip. My friend, Claude Kirkland, was also on the team. He reminded the coach that I was still on the roster, although in a non-playing capacity. I'm absolutely sure they must have exhausted every other possibility before calling me up, but they were desperate. The coach asked and I said yes, at Claude's urging.

That simple "yes" led to one of the most embarrassing experiences of my life (at least up 'till that point.) What little golf I had played was mostly with Claude on the nine-hole Georgetown Country Club Course—the only course in town.

This was a golf facility in little more than name only when compared to the perfectly manicured layouts of today. Of the nine holes, two of them had grass greens (I believe #3 and #9). The rest of them were "sand" greens. They mixed some type oil with the sand to give it a heavier consistency. It took a right swift putt to make the ball roll through that stuff unless the green was "dragged" before you putted.

Each green had about a two and a half foot strip of wood with a square of heavy canvas attached to it. There was also a rope that served as a handle. From a little past where your ball landed (eventually) on the green, you pulled the drag to smooth out the oiled sand so your putting line would be as flat as you could get it.

Sometimes, when you were tired, or just didn't want to bother, you circled your ball at about the same distance from the hole to the track the last group of players had dragged for their putts.

Hopefully you remembered the different speed between the grass greens and the oiled sand greens. If you didn't, on numbers three or nine, your ball could end up 75 yards past the hole. To say the least, the putting strokes were considerably different for the two types of surfaces.

Who Planted That Oak Tree?

The most memorable feature of the course was a giant oak tree that guarded the right side of number one, and the right side of number nine. As you might imagine, the two holes ran parallel in opposite directions.

The person who planted that tree must have had something against people who had a slice. Twice on each nine-hole round, I put a drive right smack in the middle of that tree. Sometimes they bounced out, sometimes they didn't.

You see, the really bad thing about a tree like this is that you start out feeling great on the first hole and put your initial drive into that tree. It kinda creates a damper on your round right from the beginning.

Perhaps you recover from the first slice and do pretty good through number eight. You're feeling better about your game, but a bogey, or at least a double bogey, on the last hole would make for a pretty good day. Your last drive of the round heads directly for that oak tree again . . . Oh well!

Back to the Golf Team

I packed my golf bag, all brand new balls and all. I usually played with new balls. Sometimes they may have a cut on them, but most of the time I didn't get to keep a ball long enough for it to get old.

Arriving in Charleston, the coach decided that since I was the new person on the team, I'd tee off first on number one. As I approached that tee box, my heart sank. There were people ringed around it. They had come to support the local students. I learned later that their coach was a very popular local golfer, and lots of his friends came out for every match to give the boys a boost.

"Don't worry about it," coach said as he obviously noticed my nervousness, "just play your game."

It was pretty evident that this man didn't know what he was talking about. "Play my game!" He'd never seen me play before. All he had was Claude's word to go on. I didn't feel sorry for Claude. He always beat me, whether it be golf or ping pong or marbles. The only game I held my own in was "paper soldier sticking" (If you haven't read about this yet, you will elsewhere in the book.)

I teed up my ball, took a couple of practice swings, addressed the gleaming, white, round sphere and swung—with all my might. I might as well take a chance on getting a good one. My slice played its usual trick and I sent the ball sailing off to the right. It was heading exactly for that oak tree, but the oak tree was back in Georgetown.

"I believe that's out-of-bounds," somebody behind me said. I didn't bother to turn to look. "Hit another one."

I dug another gleaming, white, sphere out of the pocket of my small bag, even had to dig for another tee. Heaven knows where the first one went. Addressed the ball, swung the club . . . you guessed it . . . a carbon copy of the first drive. That was two in a row out of bounds.

"Try once more," the crowd encouraged. Thankfully there didn't seem to be any snickering or smirking. I think they all felt my pain.

This time I teed up the ball and adjusted my stance. I turned at about a 45 degree angle to the left—aimed for the left side of the fairway. The slice didn't work like it had on the first two tries. That ball flew straight as an arrow. Although I was in the adjoining fairway to the left of number one tee, at least I wasn't out of bounds.

On the Downhill Side

From there, my game went downhill, if you can imagine! Ended up with a 126 for the day (at least it was 18 holes.)

That night, the coach treated us to a fine seafood meal at The Fork Restaurant just North of Charleston in Mount Pleasant. The treat was certainly not because we had won the match—we lost, mostly because of me. I don't even know whether or not he had money in the golf team budget for such a feast. I think the rest of the team was so down because of my performance that he thought maybe a better-than-usual meal on the road might lift their spirits a bit.

It did mine, but I don't think you'll be surprised to learn that my career as a Winyah High Golf Team starter was over almost as quickly as it had begun. One day! From then on, I was the substitute—the non-playing substitute.

The coach didn't kick Claude off the team because of me, but I don't think he paid much attention to his recommendations after that.

Always the Same

From time to time, I continued to try my hand at the game, sometimes after as much as a 15-year layoff. People would invite me to play with them, but they never seemed to ask me twice.

Even after I retired, I called some people I know who play several times a week and told them if they ever had a free spot in the foursome, or needed someone to tour the links with them, I was available. My offer fell on deaf ears.

There was one foursome that did invite me to fill in when one of the regulars couldn't play. I thought I did pretty good, but never got a second invitation.

I found out that another acquaintance was an avid golfer. I invited myself to play with him, and I must say that we did have several matches. But suddenly it ended. He didn't call anymore, and I didn't pester him.

Then there was the husband of another friend. At my invitation, we played the local public course one day. I'd told him that any-time a member of his regular foursome couldn't play, I'd be glad to fill in. He never called.

I finally figured out what I believe the problem is. I play so badly that people who are on the course with me all of a sudden start to play down to my level! Everyone I ever played with, after just a few holes, all of a sudden started making the same mistakes that plague my game. They all see their scores skyrocket when paired with me.

I don't ask anymore. You wise up after a while and realize that you shouldn't put people on the spot by inviting yourself to play with them. I've put the clubs away in the storage room. Maybe the kids can sell them after I'm gone. Maybe the spell will then be broken and they'll belong to someone who has friends to play with. Or, maybe they'll go to someone who'll just use them to stake tomato plants.

Fore!

Chapter 13

Who Decided?

Did you ever wonder, way back when, who accepted the responsibility of making the initial decision that collards were a vegetable and not a weed?

It was because of this person's decision that today we eat collards instead of honeysuckle, for that initial decision classified honeysuckle as not a vegetable.

Whoever did this deciding really cost me a bundle of money. If honeysuckle were a vegetable, I'd be able to feed my family all they wanted and still have enough left over to fill up several stalls at the Farmer's Market. And this all from a homesite that consists of about 1/2 acre, of which the house occupies about half the land.

In addition to the collard-honeysuckle decision, had the right choice been made by this early decider, I would also have been able to have an adjoining stall of dandelion and crab grass at the market. This would have insured our financial status of being healthy, wealthy members of the community.

On What Was the Decision Based?

Did you ever notice how hard it is to cultivate the things you want to have growing in your yard, and how the things you don't want growing there really thrive—even on a steady diet of weed killer chemicals?

After much research and experimentation, I think I've finally figured out the factors that went into making those early decisions that affect our life on a daily basis. Things which grow where we don't want them to grow are classified as weeds. Things which don't grow where we want them to grow are called either vegetables or flowers.

Because of these early determinations, those of us who live in houses are expected to have green, well-manicured lawns of grass. Grass does not come under the classification of "weed", therefore it

58

does not want to grow in yards—only in flower beds, which are supposed to be reserved for flowers.

Grass in flower beds is thus in the category of being a "rebellious non-weed" since it grows quite unattended in flower beds, yet refuses to grow, even when great care is extended it, in yards.

Grass will even grow on the concrete of walkways and driveways. It will cross great expanses of this rock-hard material as it heads for flower beds. Flower beds which contain the same soil that is found in the middle of the yard where it steadfastly refuses to grow.

I have even seen it thrive on brick walls, and on the trunks of pine trees, growing ever skyward with enthusiasm, while it shows disdain for top soil.

A Determination

Since "green" and "well-manicured" are the two phrases that are supposed to describe the well-kept yard, why then is it necessary to include that other word—"grass" in the description?

I have reached the decision that my lawn will be "green" and "well-manicured," even though it consists primarily of weeds. From the street, you can hardly tell the difference between close-cut, green weeds and close-cut, green grass. Therefore, I will no longer worry about the "grass" part, so long as the color is green.

After all, it has taken me many years to get these weeds to their current state of development. I am proud of them, and what's more, they don't require fertilizer. They are considerably cheaper to maintain.

If any of you reach this same conclusion, I will be happy to share. I will provide you with all the weed "cuttings" you would like to have so that you can also start having a "green" and "well-manicured" lawn.

Arise homeowners! Who needs Centipede or Bermuda or Zoysia when you have an unlimited supply of dandelions, crab grass and honeysuckle?

Chapter 14

Did Your First Car Need Shoe Tongue Leather Too?

I really haven't had much luck with cars all my life. To give you the perfect example, let me tell you about the first new one I ever bought.

When I graduated from college, received my commission as an Ensign in the Navy, I was assigned to a ship in Norfolk. The first thing that entered my mind was the need for a new car so I could go home and visit Joyce and my folks on weekends.

It was about an eight-hour drive one way, so you can easily see I needed a NEW car. Well, I went shopping in Norfolk and bought my first unused vehicle—a 1957 Chevrolet. Now, you may think this was a good choice, because you are aware the 1957 Chevrolet BelAir, eight-cylinder, hardtop model went on to become one of the world's great classic cars. It's worth much more today than it was new.

Following my usual flawed method of making a choice, I opted for the little-bit-cheaper, six-cylinder, Model 210. Right, the one that had a door post, not as nice an interior and didn't have the shiny, metal insert in that chrome flare on the rear quarter panels.

Does that tell you something about cars and me?

And to further enhance the supposition about my lack of luck in the automotive field, my new 1957 Chevy Model 210 developed a leak in the transmission on my first trip home, three days after I had purchased it. By the time I got there it was dry as a bone. Spent that entire weekend trying to get my transmission replaced so I could report back to the ship on Monday morning.

I've got to admit, however, that '57 Chevy turned out to be a good investment. Never had any more trouble with it after the second transmission was installed. I used it to teach Joyce how to drive, and it served us well for many, many years.

Real Admiration

I loved my Daddy's old early '40s Chevrolet because it had a running board on which I could stand and ride when we were visiting in the country. The main disadvantage was that it had a vacuum gear shift on the steering column. Two hands were required for a change of gears. I was broken hearted when the newer model we finally got after the war didn't have a running board, but the gear shift was a little easier to work.

My uncle was one of the first to get one of those cars where you didn't have to use the clutch all the time to change gears. I believe they called it "Fluid Drive," and we all thought that would be the thing to have—until he told us how much it cost. That was the end of that. We marveled because we didn't know he was that well off!

I remember once, in pre-driver's-license-days, someone abandoned an old coupe, with a rumble seat, in front of our house on Highway 17 in Georgetown. It was painted yellow and red, with a red dash board and yellow knobs on everything. After several days, I got the courage to sit in it and pretend to drive. I fantasized for days about having my own car and trips I would take, hoping against hope that the owner would never return and one day there would be a knock on the door. It would be the police telling me that no one had ever claimed the car, and since it had been in front of my house so long, I could have it.

Instead, one day when I got home from school, someone had towed the car off and I never saw it again.

My Very Own

The first car I was able to buy was a 1937 Chevrolet coupe. I believe it also had a rumble seat. It would run, but it used about as much oil as it did gas, and the oil dripped all the time. A friend told me that if I took some pieces of leather shoe tongue, cut a slit in each end, put one slit over the post of the spark plug and insert the spark plug cap through the other end and arrange them so the spark would have to jump about a quarter inch from the post to the cap—that would keep the plugs hot enough to burn the oil as it was pumped up around the plugs and keep the car from making such a mess.

This I dutifully did. It worked! Then I made arrangements with Vonnie, at Tiller's Gulf station on the corner of our block, to get a steady supply of used motor oil. I was in business. The only problem was that car engine sounded just like a loud sewing machine. I had the most identifiable car in town—people didn't even have to see the car to know it was me. All they had to do was listen.

Continuing the Saga

In college, my cousin who worked in the car business helped me find a 1949 Ford that was in pretty good shape, but it needed a paint job. People at the paint shop told me that either black or white were the two best colors I could select, so I said paint the body black and the top white. I later found out they had a surplus of two colors of paint—black and white.

I thought my car looked pretty spiffy when I picked it up, but when I drove out to Columbia College to get Joyce for a ride, she laughed and didn't want to get in it. "It looks like a police car," she said, "I don't think I want to ride in that."

Anyway, she finally overcame her anxiety and we dated in that car for several years.

I Play the Benevolent Brother

My little brother, Alan, didn't have a car. He had his driver's license, but no wheels. In an act of extreme love, I decided I would purchase one for him. Don't get me wrong—I wasn't independently wealthy, but I did find a great bargain.

It was an old 1949 Buick Roadmaster. Even way back then, this car was OLD! How would I describe it? Well, it was big and black and had enough chrome on it to light up the entire town of Georgetown by reflection when there was a full moon shining. It had four doors, and to my way of thinking, all of Alan's major friends could fit into it at the same time. His minor friends could fit into the trunk.

This thing was a tank! The motor purred like a kitten. Well, to be truthful, more like a lion. It probably burned a half-gallon of gas idling between cycles at the stop light.

Alan kinda half-way said "thank you," under his breath. It sure did make me feel good to be able to give it to him, but to this day I don't know whether or not he ever forgave me for the selection I made for his first vehicle. I gathered that it was not his idea of the ideal set of wheels for an up and coming Winyah High schooler.

I still think that car was a real beauty. I'd love to have it today— no computers, no pollution control devices—it was all CAR!

I Really Fell for This One

When Joyce and I came back to Columbia after the Navy, I found a small station wagon. We needed a second car for me to drive to work and this one seemed to fill the bill. It was made by the manufacturer of a very famous imported sports car. The station wagon was one of the earlier compact cars made for more than two people. It looked pretty good to me, although I don't ever remember seeing another one. That should have told me something.

I made arrangements with the bank to finance it, and on the way home I kept hearing a "clanking" sound. Maybe it was like metal hitting the pavement. A car pulled up beside me and motioned for me to roll down the window.

"You've been dropping car parts all along the street," he said sympathetically. "I looked in the rear view mirror and sure enough I could see several just in the last block. I thanked him and turned around to retrace my route. He never knew how thankful I was that he didn't laugh out loud.

In the seven or eight blocks back to the bank, I guess I picked up eight or ten pieces of metal auto parts—most of which I couldn't identify. Bad part about it, I never could find the guy I bought the car from. He had cash in hand and he was gone. I had to pay to have it fixed. I say "fixed," but that's somewhat of a misnomer. I got it so it would run, sometimes. I never did get it fixed.

One More Time...

I had one other real bad car experience with a two-year-old, well-known make of car which I bought from a friend. He had gotten it from a dealer, who had taken it in as a trade, for his wife, but decided to get rid of it. The car had low mileage and a great reputation, but that car (I use the term loosely) did things to me that I've never had another car do.

For instance, how often has your emergency brake cable broken? How about the trunk lock going bad; the glove compartment lock going bad; the door handle breaking on two different doors; the rear-view mirror falling off; spark plug cables going bad every few months; alternator, fuel pump, water pump, radiator hose and fan belt having to be replaced—all within a three-months period and then the speedometer cable going bad. The last time I tried to check the oil, the hood latch cable came out in my hand when I pulled on it. That was the last straw.

My friend felt bad about the situation, but then it was MY car!

By the way, you happen to need a car? I'm in a situation right now where I've got a couple I need to get rid of. If you're interested, I'll make you a great deal!

Chapter 15

Peanut Memories

One of the characters I remember most from my childhood was Alec, the peanut man. Alec worked the corner on the block where I lived. His regular stand was in front of Tiller's Gulf Station at the corner of Fraser and Highmarket.

He was a fixture there for so many years. When he wasn't on duty (he'd take a day off every now and then), the corner wasn't the same. It seemed empty. This kind, happy black man was always smiling, always had a kind word and a handshake for everyone he met. Let me tell you my childhood recollections of him.

Alec walked with a slight limp, and had an arm that was smaller and weaker than the other. It was fine, however, for holding up the basket that contained the brown-paper bags of peanuts. He'd put his weak arm through the handle, then tuck it tightly against his side. The usual costume, come to think of it I don't believe I ever saw him in anything else, was Oshkosh Overalls, plaid shirt and a straw hat.

He talked constantly—didn't make much difference whether or not anyone was there to hear him. He talked to every car that passed by. Most of the drivers waved or honked their horns. Sometimes this was a signal as to how many bags they wanted.

Right Through the Window

As for regular customers, they'd slow down slightly as they passed by or made the turn, window rolled down. Alec would toss the required number of bags deftly through the open window. He never missed. If you turned that corner with your window down, you got a bag of peanuts. No money changed hands at the time of delivery. Alec kept the running tab for each customer in his mind. Friday was "settle-up" day. They'd stop the car on Fridays, get their daily supply and pay their tab.

I don't know of anyone who ever argued about the tab. Alec was always right. I also never heard of anyone who tried to beat him out of the money they owed him. Alec was the Peanut Man of Georgetown, the supplier, the source. If you wanted peanuts, you got them from him.

He always had parched peanuts, but during the season when the fresh crop of green goobers were in season, I seem to remember you had a choice of parched or boiled. We always got boiled when he had them.

Alec was great with children. He made them feel as if they were the most important people in the world. He'd ignore adults when a young customer was around. I've seen some regulars have to take a turn around the block because Alec was busy with a kid. When they came by again, he'd deliver.

Peanuts! Peanuts! Get Your Boiled Peanuts...

I tried hawking boiled peanuts, and even though I was nowhere near the salesman that Alec was, I had the advantage of working a captive market! I was smart enough not to challenge him on his own turf. The Gerogetown franchise belonged to him. My selling grounds were some 30 miles up the road.

Uncle Fred lived in Hemingway, and he grew peanuts. His two sons, Walker and Carl did a lot of the harvesting, some of the boiling and all the selling. All of it, that is, except when I was visiting. They allowed me to join the team when I showed up.

We worked the tobacco markets. One thing we learned early was that people who grow, sell and buy tobacco are boiled peanut addicts. We just strolled around with our baskets and it seemed that everyone who walked up to us was holding out their hand with money in it.

If we ever had any of our supply left over, we'd head to downtown Hemingway after the markets finished up and get rid of the rest of them there. Most of the time, the downtown customers were the same ones we'd sold to earlier at the markets. They came there to shop and load up with groceries after the sale, and were usually ready for another bag to eat on the way home.

Boiling Was the Best Part

I probably liked boiling the peanuts better than I did selling them. Cooking was not difficult, but you had to learn to let them sit in the salt water long enough after they were done to soak up the required amount of salt. Improperly salted peanuts were not looked on with kindness by true devotees.

There was only one way to tell if the nuts were done, and if they were salty enough. That was to taste them, and taste them and taste them some more. Sometimes it took a while for us to determine whether or not they were at that precise, ultimate point of taste perfection.

Packaging was another precise requirement. We didn't have staples, and buying rubber bands would have been an added expense. Boiled peanuts, if they're prepared right, are always a bit moist. That made the brown, paper bags a bit damp and easy to handle. If you filled them to a certain point, you had enough bag left to fold it over a couple of times and then twist each corner so that each side had what looked like a little pig's ear sticking up.

When people saw our distinct bags, they knew exactly where the product came from, and they knew the nuts would be the best!

Next to boiling, the next favorite part of the process was getting to keep part of the proceeds. Of course we had to pay expenses, but we made good money.

I still like boiled peanuts. When I wash them, boil them, salt them down and finally take them out of the pot ready to eat, I think back to those days of peanut economy and I feel like heading for the tobacco markets with my basket.

Chapter 16

The Peddlin' Dentist

As a child, I loved the dentist, but I sure hated going to him. He was a very elderly gentleman, always happy and laughing. My Mother said he'd been her dentist every since before she and Daddy had moved to Georgetown.

"He's good, but he practices the old fashioned way," she told me. "Besides, he doesn't charge as much as the younger dentists."

By saying that he "practicing the old fashioned way," what she really meant was that he relied on the dental tools I think he must have gone into practice with the day he hung out his shingle for the first time.

"Don't need one of those new fangled electric drills," he'd tell you as he stomped a few times on the foot-peddle power source of his dentist-driven drill to see if the cable was still working properly. "It's slow, but you can really dig right down into that tooth and get out all the part that's gone bad."

When the dentist was pumping as hard as he could, it seemed that drill bit was barely turning. One of the major problems was that he liked to talk to you while he was working. Of course, even my dentist today is the same way. I think they all are. Maybe they're taught in dental school that if they try to engage you in conversation, or just rattle on by themselves, that it might take your mind off what they're doing a little bit.

Our old-timer, however, had the bad habit of slowing down his pumping when he really got a good story going. That meant the drill turned fewer and fewer rpms every second, and it took him longer and longer to excavate that cavity. The drilling time was directly related to the length of the story.

Short Term Patient

He was a jolly old gentleman, good natured to the point of pouring it on a bit too thick at times. He'd hug you and pat your shoulder, and your head, and your arm, and your cheek. Always had a joke for you. Some of them were about as old as he was.

They talked about one new woman patient who came to his office for her first visit with no advanced warning at all about his sunny disposition. He led her to the chair, which was also not new—used a hand pump to get it into position.

As she sat down, he introduced himself, asked what her problem was, then promptly asked her to remove her left shoe. He'd do things like that to break the ice, maybe take your mind off what was going to happen next.

She looked a bit puzzled, but removed the shoe as he had directed.

"Fine," he praised her, "now take off your right shoe." He pumped a couple of times on the drill pedal touched the point of the drill to his finger. "Ouch," he said teasingly.

The new patient had had enough. She bolted out of the chair, picked up her left shoe and hobbled out of the office on one stocking foot and one shoe.

He laughed as he quickly moved after her, explaining that he was just kidding. But it was too late. She never came back.

Modern Practitioners

The new woman patient probably found one of the new practitioners in town who did believe in modern equipment and electric drills, and who let his patients keep their shoes on.

I don't know whether or not The Peddlin' Dentist ever did go modern. He was a good, if old fashioned, practitioner. Even when we had to start going to someone else, someone younger, they never had to redo any of his work. It may have been slow, but he really drilled out all the bad stuff before he put the filling in.

I do think, however, that my dread of going to the dentist to this day stems from the hard-grinding, slow motion of that foot-peddle driven drill. Even when they crank up those high speed, almost-painless grinders of today, I still look down to see if the dentist is pumping with his foot.

Chapter 17

Don't Ask for Cornbread in a Real Chinese Restaurant

I came to Columbia in August, 1953 to go to college at the University of South Carolina and get my education—a small-town boy from Georgetown in the big city with its big city ways. I had a lot to learn about lots of things. Looking back on the experience, I did OK in some areas, in others my learning was woefully lacking.

It was shortly after arriving that I got my first taste of Chinese food. That has proven to be one of the more positive aspects of my education.

During my childhood and teenage years, I didn't miss many meals, as the old saying goes. Raised on a steady diet of fresh vegetables, lots of potatoes, beef, pork, chicken and fish, with a smattering of wild game including squirrel, duck, game birds—my eating habits pretty much covered the Southern food spectrum.

I quickly learned there were lots of dishes quite foreign to me, however. The only Italian cuisine I had ever consumed was spaghetti, served at the school lunch room far too often! It took me a long time to get over that "culinary delight" and reach the point where I could go out to a authentic Italian restaurant and at least read the menu without those terrible thoughts returning.

Chinese was also completely foreign to me. There weren't any such restaurants in Georgetown. Our top culinary experience was the Gladstone Hotel that served red rice and duck, very highly spiced, on Saturdays. Next to that was the Whistling Pig which is gone now but still in my memory had the best hot dogs with chili I've found in my travels to many parts of the world. They toasted the bun, frank and chili in one of those toasters that mashed the bread flat.

70

First Date

There was one Chinese restaurant in Columbia that my friends had recommended. Perhaps even more outstanding in my memory than the fact that the food was supposed to be good, was that the cost was very minimal for the amount you got.

I truly believe it was probably for this reason that one of the first dates Joyce and I had was a visit to Kester's Bamboo House in Five Points. She was a student at Columbia College, from the semi-big city of Florence. I didn't know whether or not they had any Chinese restaurants there, but I thought it might impress her if I took her out for Chinese. It sure did impress me!

Kester's was rather dimly lit, but you could still pick out the features that said: "Hey, we're different. We're oriental. See the paper lanterns, the gold dragons, the red and gold and black motif. Hear that different, twangy music?"

I guess Joyce and I quickly became addicts. Seems that I remember the menu there was somewhat a mixture of Americanized Chinese, with a sprinkling of dishes that could have been somewhat authentic. Kester was certainly not a Chinese name. But the food was good, the prices right, and there was a bit of atmosphere.

Across the Continent to China Town

After college and marriage, Joyce and I were stationed in San Francisco for a year when my ship, the USS Ranger (CVA-61) moved from Norfolk, Virginia, to Alameda, California. That's another story. When I got my commission, I asked for a small ship in the Atlantic. The Navy put me on an aircraft carrier in the Pacific! Welcome to the military.

One of our first outings in the big city by the bay was to China Town where we got to eat real Chinese food in a real Chinese restaurant. At Kester's, we had specialized in combination platters where you got portions of three our four different menu items. This genuine oriental restaurant didn't have combination meals.

There were so many things on the menu we wanted to try that we went a bit wild in our ordering. Not realizing that each item we ordered seemed to be designed for a family serving, when they brought our food from the kitchen they had to pull up an extra table to our booth so they'd have room to put all the food.

We were embarrassed. The waiters smiled knowingly at the two Southerners. In the end, I think even they were surprised at the dent we put in those servings. They stood aside and watched, and smiled a knowing "look-at-the-hicks-smile." They nodded and whispered to each other in that beautiful sing-song language as we sampled each different dish. We smiled too! We asked for a doggie bag so we could take the leftovers home. It took more than one bag.

During our stay in the San Francisco area, we visited China Town many times, but we did tone down our ordering practices just a bit. We tried different restaurants, but usually returned to that first one. The waiters smiled when they saw us coming, and you could tell they always reminded each other of our first visit when they had to pull up that extra table.

Buffets

Our culinary delight in Oriental food has not changed over the years, though our taste buds have branched out a bit to include more Italian dishes, and occasionally Tex-Mex. We still eat Chinese at least once a week.

Columbia, like most cities, now probably has as many or more Chinese restaurants than any other single type eatery. The big attraction is the buffet. Our newest advertises 120 different items from which to choose. Years ago, Joyce and I would have probably tried to sample all 120 at one sitting, but our experiences have encouraged us to spread out such a sampling over several visits.

There are some who don't care for buffets. They prefer the restaurants that individually cook each dish when ordered—think they're "more elite." They don't consider Chinese buffets to be "real Chinese." I don't hold that against them though.

Perhaps some would say that going to a Chinese buffet is going second class. Well, I guess second class describes us. We do enjoy the tremendous spread and all its different selections. It's like a giant combination plate!

Let me quickly add, however, that we also enjoy the "more elite" Chinese gastronomic palaces that don't have a buffet.

You see, there're all kinds, just like people. For years our favorite Chinese house of marvelous eating had Mexican cooks. It was not unusual to find real out-of-place dishes on their buffet. No, not Mexican menu items, rather things like macaroni and cheese, French fries, hot bar-b-qued chicken wings, peach cobbler.

One of the newer buffets here routinely features hash-browned potatoes, cherry tomatoes, cheesecake, fried catfish nuggets. I think when they reach 120 or more different items, maybe they have to stretch things a bit and throw in a few FOREIGN dishes to reach that fantastic total.

Good Gravy

I like the gravy featured in so many dishes. That delicious, dark-brown liquid of the peppered steak and so many other mixed meat and vegetable dishes. My wife says I should call it sauce—not gravy.

One of the disadvantages to eating Chinese is that not very much of this gravy sticks to anything. You pick up a piece of bell pepper and not much gravy comes with it. Chicken and beef attract a little more, but still not much. You're always left with lots of good, brown gravy floating around in your plate.

Egg Foo (or as I've also seen it on some menus—Fu) Young is one of our favorites. Sometimes I cover it with that thick, light-brown SAUCE, sometimes I don't. To tell you the truth, I think I would enjoy the gravy, or sauce, even more if I could find a piece of cornbread somewhere on that 120-choice buffet to go with the meal.

What Do You Sop With?

Chinese evidently don't go in much for bread. They have those little fried pieces of sweet donut dough, but to an old Southerner, bread you eat with your meal isn't sweet. True, some of us do put a bit more sugar in cornbread than we should, but biscuits and rolls and sourdough and light bread aren't sweet.

Can you imagine how much better the Chinese dining experience would be if you had a piece of cornbread to sop up that left over gravy? You can't sop gravy with that sweet, fried bread. Sometimes it even has powdered sugar on it. Powdered sugar-covered-fried-sweet-bread does not go well with brown gravy.

I wonder if Chinese folks really know what they're missing when they don't serve cornbread with their meals? Surely they've never tried it. I'll bet it would only take once and they'd be hooked.

Four Different Kinds!

I've toyed with the idea of opening up my own Chinese. In addition to my favorites like General Tao's Chicken, Egg Foo Young, fried Catfish Nuggets, Broccoli Chicken, Egg Rolls, French Fried Potatoes, Battered Shrimp, Boneless Chicken, Sweet and Sour Chicken, Egg Drop Soup and about 110 additional items—I'd have FOUR KINDS OF CORNBREAD.

First would be regular, old, yellow cornbread cooked in a cake, just a pinch of sugar if any at all. The Chinese don't seem to appreciate butter either, so we'd have to add some butter to go with the bread. I guess if you don't have real bread with your meal, there's no reason to have real butter!

Then there'd be Mexican Cornbread with lots of Jalapeno peppers and some whole-kernel corn—kinda spicy. Any good Chinese buffet would also have to have some Cracklin' Cornbread, chock full of those bits of hog skin that melt in your mouth—not the hard, crunchy kind.

Last on the list would be Hushpuppies, delicately fried-to-a-golden-brown nuggets of finely-ground corn meal, with chopped-up sweet onions floating in the soupy meal. Plopped into fresh, bubbling vegetable oil or peanut oil (in the old days I would have preferred pig lard), and of such consistent consistency they would automatically turn themselves to cook evenly. Can you imagine a more complimenting offering to accompany Chinese brown gravy?

I've mentioned this to several Chinese proprietors. Their usual reaction is to smile knowingly, nod their head, say something in almost English that I can't understand, and then ask me: "How was everything tonight?" That usually comes out more understandable that the reply to my cornbread question.

Still, if they can add fried catfish nuggets, hash-brown potatoes, macaroni and cheese, cheesecake and Oreo ice cream to their REAL CHINESE BUFFET, what could possibly be their aversion to cornbread?

I guess it must be something in the cultural differences of the races. It really must be something deeply ingrained in their culinary history. Even the younger Chinese who have adopted so many American customs like blue jeans and rock and roll or heavy metal music seem to have avoided cornbread.

Tell me truthfully now. In all your Chinese dining experiences, even in those restaurants in small southern towns too small to have a McDonald's or Hardee's, but still have Oriental, have you ever come across a real Chinese menu that contained cornbread?

If you've ever traveled to the real China, or been invited to a meal in a Chinese home in America—cornbread?

See!

Chapter 18

Is it True? Are They Devil Cats?

Remember that old superstition about black cats crossing your path? I've always wondered how it affected other people who own black cats.

We've had two in our family, and I found them to be nothing more than loving, affectionate animals. No evidence of them being "witches' cats," or causing bad luck, or anything like that. No bad omens or supernatural happenings. Just a superstition.

But the other day, when I was out driving, SOMEBODY ELSE'S black cat ran across the road in front of me. Two blocks later, the timing belt on my engine just came apart . . .

Other Cats I've Known

My daughter had an ATTACK CAT! No kidding, when this cat was young, she was one of the meanest animals I've ever come across. She had to be locked in the bedroom when company came. Then she'd promptly attack my daughter when let out of the lockup.

Murphy was always an inside cat, and I must admit she mellowed in her old age. She had to be declawed (front claws only) to keep her from tearing up all the furniture, but since she didn't have to fight for her life outside, that fact didn't seem to bother her too much.

Along with the mellowing came another couple of habits. She talked to my daughter all the time, especially when she was on the telephone. Murphy hated for her to be on the telephone. She literally screamed at her—tried to hang up the phone, pulled on her arm, bit her leg. Yes, she still had her teeth. It was only the claws that she lost.

Murphy also lived in the house with Mr. Kitty. This is a kind, gentle, loving cat whom Murphy learned to tolerate. Mr. Kitty came to the home long after Murphy had established control of the household.

They both loved to sleep atop the ironing board, each laid claim to one end of the padded surface. Every now and then, one would decide to explore the other's end of the board. "Incidents" were known to take place when this happened.

Unpretty Dogs

If one daughter can claim the meanest cat, the other can claim the unprettiest (I won't say ugly because they're good at heart) two small dogs I believe I've ever come across. Punkie has passed on, but leaves behind the picture of being Phyllis Diller's early years' hairdo running around on four short legs. Much of Punkie's hair was missing, but what was there stood straight up and out in all directions.

Rabbit is still with us. She's a brown, softer hair version of Punkie, but not at all pretty. But she is loved—they were both loved very much.

I guess I should apologize to the family for calling them unpretty. I'll change that to read: "they were so unattractive they would have to be classified as cute."

Chapter 19

All About Coons 'N Biscuits 'N Tabasco Sauce

Small game hunting and fishing were my dad's strong points, and I've always been thankful that he took the time to teach me. However, the one thing I didn't inherit was his love of coon hunting.

Sure, as a youngster, I stumbled along through the woods and the swamps on a few dark, cold nights; and I tried my best to cultivate an excitement for hearing the "music" of those dogs barking. But I never did come to appreciate it the way he did.

My Dad and Davis were a pair made for coon hunting. They could listen and tell you from a mile or more away exactly what the dogs were doing and where they were doing it. At times, they could even identify in which tree a dog had finally chased a coon, and which dog had treed first.

"Ole Herman's got that coon up that hollow hickory down by Haselden's Landing," one would say, and the other would quickly agree. "Listen to that music, son. Did you ever hear anything richer than 'Ole Herman's voice when he's treed? Let's go to 'em!"

Dad and Davis went way back as a team. Davis was not only a distant cousin, but a boyhood pal as well. Some said that about as high as his ambition ever reached was to hope for three or four coons in one night. He'd eat the meat and sell the hides to supplement his meager earnings from sharecropping the small farm in which Dad was part owner. But he was about as happy a fellow as I've ever run across.

My First Hunt

The first time I ever went into the woods with them at night, I remember not being able to figure out how a fellow could be so happy to be going hunting and he didn't even get to carry a gun.

But that was Davis. To me the gun was the symbol of manliness and the real meaning of going on the hunt. Sling it over your shoulder and be ready to lower the boom on whatever game presented itself, be it a coon or a possum.

Those were the days, though, when hunters such as Davis were out to put meat on the table to feed their families. Sure, they enjoyed the thrill of the chase and the howl of the hounds, but it went much deeper than that. Who shot wasn't important. What was important was that he shot well. It often meant eating or not eating.

Dad and Davis had a standard arsenal they took on every coon hunt. It consisted of one aged, short-barreled, single-shot, bolt-cocking, 22 rifle with a hair trigger and a sight that must have been made out of coon magnets. To supplement the arsenal, each took a flashlight (which their pride prevented being turned on to see where they were going unless it was a dire necessity). Flashlights were really only for shining the coon's eyes.

They also carried an ax that was used on more than one occasion to chop down a hollow tree and get the coon out of a hole, and a few kitchen matches to start a fire to stand by while you listened to the dogs trail.

Since I made such a fuss over it, they always let me carry the rifle, although I was seldom entrusted with the task of shooting the coon.

On The Other Side

There were a lot of things I never understood about coon hunting, not the least being why a coon could never be treed on this side of the water. More than one night, I came back colder and more miserable than was necessary because we had to cross a branch or a swamp to get to the coon.

I also never understood why the dogs were able to strike a new trail just about the time when Dad and Davis seemed ready to call it quits for the night. The highlight of every coon hunt, as far as I was concerned, was when it was over. I looked forward to getting back to Davis' house and being able to stretch my cold feet out on the earthen hearth in front of a roaring fire while waiting for his wife, Ethel, to fix us something to eat.

Since Davis and Ethel often had trouble putting enough food

on the table for their family, I knew Dad used to slip him a few dollars after every hunt to help take care of what we ate. I often wondered what Ethel might have been able to produce if she'd had a fully equipped kitchen and all the ingredients she wanted to work with. Instead she only had a wood stove, well water and meager supplies. She was still some cook.

I'm about to make a confession to you. Ethel cooked coon and I ate in on more than one occasion. And it was GOOD.

Did you ever notice how people who enjoy venison and rabbit and even squirrel can look down their noses something fierce at you if you admit you like to eat coon? Another confession—possum wasn't too bad either the way Ethel hashed it up, though I'd probably deny ever tasting it if the question came up in a crowd.

Yeap, the standard fare after one of those coon hunts was coon and homemade biscuits and baked sweet potatoes. To this day, those were the best biscuits I've ever eaten in all this world. What Ethel produced from flour and lard and unpasteurized milk would literally melt in your mouth. These were real CHOLESTEROL-ENHANCED biscuits—none of that stuff that's pre-packaged and talks to you on the way to the oven.

These things you find in the dairy case today where you peel off the foil wrapped from the outside of the cylinder, pop the rest of the cardboard on the edge of the counter and the dough comes oozing out to be put in the pan and slid into a preheated oven—they couldn't come close to Ethel's creations. She made the real thing, and I wish I had one of them today, even though it'd probably send my cholesterol off the chart.

No Butter Needed

You really didn't need any butter on her biscuits. The animal fat took care of that, but she always seemed to come up with a little butter to go on the baked, piping-hot sweet potatoes. When you broke the skin, you had to duck the steam that came pouring out.

And the coon—the piece de resistance! She would boil it for hours, on top of the wood stove, with plenty of salt and pepper. Then she'd chop it up into little pieces and brown it in the oven 'til it was so crispy it would crunch when you spooned it out of the pan onto your plate.

You'd have been hard pressed back during those days to convince me that Davis and Ethel were underprivileged. Anybody who could eat like this every time I came to hunt, who didn't have to keep regular work hours, and who could go hunting or fishing about any time they darn well pleased, seemed quite well off to me.

As I grew older, I think I came to understand more and more why what other people considered a lack of ambition on Davis' part didn't really seem to concern him at all.

One night after we'd finished eating, Dad and Davis were outside skinning the coons the hunt had produced. I propped my still-damp feet up in front of the fire, and Ethel brought me another biscuit and a steaming cup of coffee. The smile on here face told me she knew how much I appreciated the attention.

"Miss Ethel, I wish I could eat your biscuits all the time. Davis sure is a lucky fellow," I told her. I cradled the cup in my still-cold hands and savored the mixed aroma of the coffee and the mouthwatering biscuit offering she'd presented me.

"Davis likes my biscuits too," she beamed as she watched me take a bite. "He says they're his favorite, even when we got no coon and sweet potatoes."

A Confidence

She confided to me that night that Davis' favorite snack of all time was when she came up with a little extra money to be able to splurge on a bottle of Tabasco Sauce. "I'll make him up a batch of half-dozen biscuits or so, and he'll sit there and drench them one by one in that hot sauce 'til he's lapped up every crumb of bread and every drop of sauce. He really likes that, and seeing him enjoy it so much makes me feel good too."

As a youngster, I heard some people snicker at Davis behind his back. But can you tell me that a man who is satisfied going hunting without carrying a gun, who takes care of his family as best he can, and whose favorite meal in all the world is animal fat biscuits soaked in hot sauce, and who could care less what other people think about the way he lives his life—isn't the picture of happiness?

Valuable Lessons

No, Dad and Davis didn't ever teach me to like coon hunting the way they did, but they did provide a philosophy by which I try to live.

First, they showed me that simple things can be mighty rewarding.

Secondly, they taught me that every man's ambition is the direct results of his own expectations, and that is what's important. In a subtle way, they taught me not to be too quick in judging others. They advanced the philosophy that the determination of whether an individual is successful or not is really nobody else's business.

Davis didn't have much, but he didn't expect someone else to take care of him either. He made do, and was happy with, whatever he was able to get on his own.

Finally, they made me understand that you don't always have to carry the gun to be the big cheese.

They're both gone now, but to this day I can't come face to face with a bottle of Tabasco Sauce without smiling. A tear comes to my eyes and my heart longs for the good 'ole days when biscuits were real biscuits, and two of the world's greatest success stories at least gave me the chance to learn to love coon hunting.

(First published in *South Carolina Wildlife* Magazine)

Chapter 20

Is Fat Fatter Than it Used to Be?

"Looks like that cholesterol is a bit too high. Have we been watching it?" the doctor asked. I don't know whether he was asking for my benefit or his. "You need to cut down on the fat portion of your diet. We'll recheck it the next time you're in."

I knew what the answer was, but I figured that's what I was paying him for. Never mind the fact it was for my own good. He told me the same thing the last time I was in for a checkup. I guess he didn't read all my file.

I really try not to eat that much fat, but it seems like my will-power gets less and less with each passing day—especially when I'm confronted with a buffet. They put a single serving plate before me and I know I'm pretty much limited to that much food, but tell me I can "eat all I want" and I feel obligated to try.

Perhaps It's Inherited

All four of my grandparents were "grand" eaters. I remember some of those tables we sat down to, especially Thanksgiving, Christmas or any excuse for a holiday, and I tell you they'd put most modern-day buffet, eat-all-you-want restaurants, to shame.

My grandparents on Mother's side of the family owned a general store in Hemingway, and in addition had a tremendous farm. They raised cattle and hogs and all the grain to feed them, plus their own vegetables.

They had a smokehouse as big as our living room. It was right outside the kitchen door, and to this day I sometimes dream about all those hams and shoulders and slab bacon hanging from hooks in the ceiling, on the side walls, even on the posts that supported the roof. There were pork skins and cracklins', fatback and streak-o-lean, smoked link sausage, dried onions and peppers. It was a gastronomic sight.

For those of you who don't know, streak-o-lean is fat back with a little streak of lean meat running through it. Fatback is

100 percent fat—no lean at all.

Many's the time I ate a meal where fatback or streak-o-lean was the meat course. It went great with sweet potatoes and grits and just about anything. Sometimes there would be two meat courses, perhaps pork chops with fatback on the side, or fried chicken or fried steak with fatback. As far as steak was concerned, the best part of the meat to all of them was the juicy fat around the outside of the piece.

In addition to eating it fried, they flavored everything on the table with fatback. Big slabs of it were tossed in with collard, mustard or turnip greens. Black-eyed peas, green beans, field peas, okra all were made better because of fatback.

Great Biscuits

The best biscuits in the world are made with lard, not vegetable oil, but animal lard. Probably my total daily quota of cholesterol today would have been contained in one half of one of those biscuits. Then, on top of that, we loaded them down with real butter.

We put butter on corn on the cob, pancakes, cornbread—double butter on grits, and sometimes even on rice.

Then for desert we'd have apple pie, the crust made with animal fat, and topped with real, heavy whipped cream! Or we'd have homemade pound cake with a week's supply of table butter in it.

As I grew older and didn't visit with the grandparents so much, I got away from some of this kind of eating. Mother followed many of the same recipes, but she didn't use quite as much lard and fatback and butter.

Watch It!

In later years, since the doctor told me in 1984 that I had to give up sugar, salt, nicotine and caffeine—all at the same time—I have tried to eat a bit more healthy food.

And now, here I am. Him asking: "have we been watching your cholesterol? We'd better start."

The ironic part—my grandparents ate like this every day of their life and they all lived long, productive lives. Some of them into their late 80s or 90s. On top of that, both of my Daddy's parents smoked corn cob pipes and dipped snuff. On Mother's side, her Father smoked a pipe and her Mother dipped snuff.

As for my Mother and Daddy, she lived to be 89 and Daddy, 82.

Evidently, cholesterol didn't have all that much effect on them. Maybe fat back then wasn't as fat as fat is today. Reckon?

But anyway, "we're watching my cholesterol now." We're also watching my blood sugar and my blood pressure.

Oh for the good 'ole days when all one had to watch was whether or not one could stand up and walk after leaving the well-endowed table.

Chapter 21

A Good Place to Live

Did you ever get the feeling that maybe you'd like to live on television? Every time I watch the tube, I get the idea that television living is ideal—same with the movies to some degree.

Life is so simple with none of those complicating, bothersome details that we have to put up with in everyday life. People on television can leave their doors and windows open and never have to worry about any bugs or insects coming in. They can fry bacon or chicken or pork chops and never have the first splash of grease splattering on the stove.

On television, the paper towels always tear off evenly, and they wipe up spills with one pass. They don't do this at my house. In fact, I've had some brands of paper towels that seem to repel water rather than absorbing it.

Pets on television never get fleas or shed hair or have to go to the bathroom. They always wait to be taken outside. Dogs never slobber or chew up the furniture. Cats never get fur balls.

On television, the cans of spray paint always spray evenly, unlike the cans I buy that always spit out those extra large blobs of paint that spot the surface something awful. On TV, the paint never runs.

On television, people can work outside in their yards without ever seeing a bug or getting bitten by a mosquito. They can even have a picnic completely free of ants and other insects. Every time I walk outside, I am immediately surrounded by a swarm of gnats having a contest to see which one can get into my eyes, nose, ears or mouth first. The gnats are quickly followed by mosquitoes, biting flies or those pesky little white flies that come from nowhere.

People on television have squirrels that don't eat their pecans and birds that don't mess on their car windows, patio furniture, outdoor grill or anywhere else they please.

On television, one coat of paint is all you need to cover a wall. When I try that one-coat paint, I still see a spot or streak or two even after the third coat. Their paint doesn't drip. Mine does, if not on me, then on the floor.

On television, there is always a parking space waiting for you, no matter where you're going. Even down town, or in front of the busiest hotel in the world, your space is there. I have to circle the block several times and then usually park two blocks away from my destination.

Clothes come out of the dryer already ironed and folded on television. My dryer doesn't work like this. My soap powder cakes and doesn't completely take out any kind of stain like theirs does.

People on television never have the embarrassment of having to go to the bathroom at an awkward time (except in a few of those upset stomach commercials, and even then there's always a facility close at hand).

When I watch programs, I never see anyone get a paper cut, or a boil, or hit their knee on the sharp corner of a desk or other piece of furniture. I've never seen them have an ingrown toenail or bite their tongue.

I rest my case. The people on television very definitely have life easier than we do. All in all, I'd say that has to be a pretty good place to live.

Chapter 22

Taking Time to be Thankful

I went out to mow the front lawn the other night. I waited until about 6:45 thinking it would have cooled off some, but the temperature was still hovering around 94 degrees with not a breath of a breeze.

I had let the grass grow far too long, and you know how it is to try to push a mower through that thick mat, even when the weather is nice and cool.

The mower choked down several times. I swallowed two bugs, and those little beetle-like things with orange stripes on their wings were constantly flying up out of the grass onto my legs and in my face. I was hot and miserable as I struggled to get the job done before it got dark.

Man, this was too much like work. I was soaking wet, and tired, and thirsty and just about to the point of throwing in the towel.

Then a gentle breeze sprang up and I looked back at the part of the yard that was finished. It sure did look a lot better than it had when I started. That, in itself, gave me the incentive I needed to complete the job.

As I sat on the trunk of the car trying to cool off, I thought back to my old yard—the one in Georgetown where I grew up. It was about 15 percent the size of this one, and the cutting implement back then was really a PUSH mower—the kind that didn't have a motor, and the horsepower that the pusher provided propelled the wheels and the blade.

"Count your blessings man! Suppose you still had that ancient relic instead of this modern push mower that at least has an engine to turn the cutting blade." Cutting the grass wasn't one of my favorite chores as a child. I had to be urged, perhaps even mildly threatened, before I sprang into action. But this grass was a bit different. It was mine. I was responsible for it. There was nobody for me to threaten. I wanted it to look nice for my family and the neighbors.

I looked at the neatly manicured, lush green lawn and took some pride in it—not the flower beds—they still needed some attention. Another thought suddenly came to me. How many people were there in this world who would love to have that grass to cut? How many people are there in this world who have the grass but aren't physically able to cut it?

This grass may not be the greatest in the world, but it's mine, and so far I'm able to take care of it. This yard may not be the greatest in the world, but it's mine and I'm proud to have it.

I guess sometimes we're all guilty of taking what we have for granted, only thinking of what the next great blessing to come along might be. We wonder what we're going to get next instead of stopping to think of the great abundance we have for which to be thankful. We look with envy at people who have more and wish we could be in their shoes.

There's an old saying that goes something like this: I felt sorry for myself because I had no shoes, until I met a man who had no feet.

I'm glad I cut the grass that particular, hot evening. I'm glad I got hot and sweaty and thirsty and miserable. I'm glad I had to take the time to cool off after I'd finished, and pause for a few moments enjoying my grass.

I hope from here on out I can take the time to enjoy some of the other many blessings I already have without being on a constant lookout for even more.

Chapter 23

Grits, Plain and Simple

I guess the first solid food I ever ate was grits. At least it seems that way.

I can't remember when it wasn't a part of my diet. My Mother was a great grits cook. Often, we'd have it for breakfast, then again for supper. She served it with lots of favorite side dishes, but the grits was always the same—creamy but not runny. You know, the kind that would stay where you put it on the plate, but it was never too firm or "pasty."

You people who don't care for grits don't know what you're missing. Don't get me wrong, I don't look down at people who think hashed brown potatoes are the desired breakfast fare over grits. They're welcomed to their preferences.

I like potatoes too—any way you can fix them. Sometimes when I go out to a breakfast buffet, they'll have grits and potatoes on the bar. I guess that's because we have so many Northerners living here now. I'm not prejudiced though. I usually eat both. I'll ladle on a spoon of hashed browns right next to my grits.

Side Dishes

I mentioned the side dishes Mother served with grits. For breakfast there'd often be the regular fare. Always eggs, and either bacon, sausage or ham. When she served ham, there'd also be red-eye gravy to go on the grits. Otherwise, just butter.

I've seen people get a bowl of grits in a restaurant and then put milk and sugar on it. This was a pretty indisputable clue that they were from somewhere else. One time, I saw a guy put chocolate syrup on grits. That was pretty hard to take, I mean even just to have to look at that. There are some Southerners, I must admit, who put catchup (or catsup or ketchup) on their grits, but not chocolate syrup!

Shad was my Dad's favorite fish. It has a rich flesh, full of little tiny "Y" bones, but properly fried, is delicious. We had shad with grits, and perhaps a baked sweet potato and cornbread.

Fried squirrel in thick, brown gravy was another supper favorite. Sometimes quail or doves would be substituted for squirrel. We didn't eat rabbit. I really don't know why, but to this day, I've never tasted rabbit.

Grits and eggs scrambled with pork brains could be either a breakfast or supper delicacy. Instead of brains, Mother would sometimes cook tripe, another family favorite.

The Real Stuff

Today we use "quick grits" that is supposed to cook in five minutes. I think the longer it cooks, the better it taste. The grits we used to have at home was usually the old fashioned, stone ground kind. You had to wash it pretty thoroughly before you cooked it. Lots of the chaff from the corn was left in after the grinding process at the mill. You had to keep covering the grits with water and let it sit long enough for the chaff to float to the top. Then you'd pour that off, fill up the bowl and repeat the process quite a few times.

This was no "five minutes" deal. I think Mother let it simmer for hours before a meal.

She loved to cook grits when we went for our vacations at Pawleys Island. They did seem to taste even better there. We'd often have them with fried Whiting or Flounder, with shrimp creole or with deviled crabs or crab cakes. She said the extra sulfur content of the beach water made the grits taste better—it even made it look a bit different.

A Grits Disaster

One night at the beach when she was cooking grits, she spilled a pot of the boiling hot substance on her leg. It just sat there and she screamed. We tried to wipe it off as best we could while Daddy ran next door to Dr. J. H. Danner's house to see if he had any burn medicine.

He was our preacher from Duncan Memorial Methodist Church in Georgetown, and I think he must have known at least something about every subject in the world.

He didn't have any medicine, but on the way out of his house he grabbed a couple of Irish potatoes. Running into the room where Mother was writhing in pain, he took a quick look, then went in the kitchen. He cut the potatoes in two, grabbed a big spoon and began scraping the potatoes into a bowl.

He put this paste on her leg and wrapped it with a wet towel. Almost immediately, the pain seemed to lessen. He let that stay on her leg for a while, then repeated the process. She was instructed to let that stay on overnight.

The next morning, she took the dressing off and her leg was just a bit red. Sometimes I still think about that accident and how painful an injury it would have been if Dr. Danner hadn't come to the rescue. Can you imagine the pain of hot boiling grits on her leg?

Now, I'm not recommending that you try this remedy for burns. I'm sure a doctor would have recommended other treatment. All I'm saying is it worked for her that summer night, and we were all thankful for a neighbor who at least had a procedure to try for the accident. Maybe it worked so well for Mother because he was our preacher and we believed in him. You know the saying, "Faith can move. . ."

Yellow Grits—Worthy Fare For Any Gourmet

Sometimes we had the luxury of yellow grits. I don't know whether or not this cost more, but we didn't have it very often. It was milled from a different kind of corn, I think, and had a distinctive taste all its own. That was a meal to remember when we had yellow grits.

Maybe it was sorta like brown eggs. Both my parents absolutely declared that brown eggs tasted better than white eggs, although a study a few years ago showed there was no difference at all in the taste or nutritional value of the two different colors. You'd have had a hard time convincing them that the people who did that study knew anything at all about eggs.

I think brown eggs have always cost more though. But anytime we had yellow grits and brown eggs, especially with country ham and red-eye gravy, that was a meal to talk about at least for the next few days.

Modern Day Miracle

I'll tell you an experience I had in later years with yellow grits. I had a photography studio in Boozer Shopping Center in Columbia and often ate at the fountain in St. Andrews Pharmacy just down the sidewalk. Charlie cooked a pretty good breakfast. Well, to really be truthful, Charlie cooked a great breakfast!

I liked his grits, and he served hot biscuits toasted in one of those toasters that "mashed things flat." I went in one day and he was serving yellow grits instead of the pale, white ones usually dished up.

I couldn't believe it. Here was one of my favorite meals from the past—yellow grits with scrambled eggs, country ham and "flat" biscuits.

I didn't miss breakfast at the Pharmacy for several months. I'd never get my fill of yellow grits. But one morning, I went in at the regular time and found Charlie rushing to get breakfast ready. There was a counter full of customers and he'd been late that morning. I took the last seat available, back by the grill where he usually sat and smoked when he had a break from cooking.

Charlie was stirring the pot full of grits. Lots of people might not realize it, but almost constant stirring is one of the secrets of great grits cooking. All of a sudden I saw him reach for the shelf and get a bottle of yellow food coloring. He opened it and started pouring that yellow liquid into the pot of grits!

My heart sank. Charlie's yellow grits was nothing but white grits with yellow food coloring in it. I believe that was as close to a food sacrilege as I've ever seen. My heart sank. The grits didn't taste the same to me that morning, or any morning thereafter. I never did quit liking his "flat" biscuits though.

Chapter 24

Finally Getting My Tax Money's Worth on Something

Sometimes I get a bit tired having to pay such high property taxes. When you get right down to it, people don't ever really own a home or an automobile or a boat or a travel trailer. They just rent them from the government—the rent payments being in the form of property taxes.

But I have to admit that there's one organization on that stub that shows me how my taxes are divided up that I don't have any complaints about paying. That's the share that goes to the County Public Library.

By using the services provided by our tax monies, I've been able to travel to far corners of not only the country, but the world. Through travel books and videos, through talking books of great reporters like Charles Kuralt, I've been able to visit countless places of my dreams.

I've been able to enjoy far more music than I could ever afford to buy for a private collection. I've been able to explore forms of music I didn't know whether or not I'd like. I've been able to visit places that I didn't know if they would appeal to me. I've been able to revisit places where I've actually been and find out how true-to-form the travel pieces were, or what I'd missed. Often I wished I'd checked out the book or tape before my visit instead of after.

Still In My Dreams

Even though I visit the library several times each week and take great joy when they get in a new offering that I haven't check out before, there are still places in my dreams. I know that it will take an actual visit, or revisit, to them before those dreams are fulfilled.

My dream places are all in the United States. I got enough foreign travel in the Navy, and although I've never been to Europe, it's not really high on my dream travels.

I'll bet you also have a list. Let's compare them:

KEY WEST

The Conch Republic has always been a dream. The Southernmost point in the United States, even though completely touristized, still has to be a romantic, beautiful destination. The fantastic sunsets, the weird mix of people who populate the area, the vast sweep of ocean and sand and blue water and blue sky—what a great combination of sights and sounds.

Having been brought up in Georgetown, where the coast and my second home of Pawleys Island were only 12 miles away, I guess I've always been a beach-and-ocean-lover. Eating seafood is one of my all-time favorite activities in the gastronomic realm. The smell of a salt-water breeze, the chattering of shore birds, the aroma of a salt-water marsh, the thrill of ocean waves, the rhythm of reeds and grasses waving from atop ever-changing dunes—the catalog of pluses could go on almost forever.

I got as far South as Miami once, but Key West has to be a different, better world. I found a lot of artificial people and places in Miami. The Conchs, for better or worse, I believe are for real. Characters certainly, but they have the convictions to live their beliefs and stick with their lifestyles.

TARPON SPRINGS

This is my second Florida dream destination. I saw a movie once set in this small seaport town which was originally populated by Greek sponge divers. There's probably more of then in the restaurant business now than the sponge business, but all the books and travel logs portray it as a small, friendly village that opens its heart to visitors of the tourist variety. I automatically love any place on or near water. Tarpon Springs certainly qualifies.

NEW ORLEANS

I've been there four or five times, from a NROTC Midshipman on my senior cruise, to a quick visit when Joyce and I were returning to South Carolina from our year-long stay in San Francisco, to business conventions and a national fishing tournament.

While I've always enjoyed the great restaurants, the food, Bourbon Street, the French Quarter, Jackson Square, etc., it was only on this last visit with the Bass Angler's Sportsman Society (BASS), that I was able to visit Preservation Hall for the first time.

Dixieland Jazz has always been my favorite music, and why I hadn't taken the time out for Preservation Hall on previous visits really blows my mind. If I ever get there again, it'll be for three reasons: camping at Preservation Hall every night to listen to the authentic Dixieland Jazz Bands; eating at as many restaurants as I can visit; and riding the river, exploring a bit of the great Mississippi.

The last time they put us up in the Hyatt Regency adjoining the Super Dome. Next time I want to be in a small hotel in the French Quarter. The only big hotel I want to visit is the one where Pete Fountain has his nightclub. I'd love to spend the $50 admission to hear Pete blow that clarinet.

NORTHERN MINNESOTA

When I was in high school, I joined my aunt and her family to visit family members who had fled Georgetown for the north woods of Minnesota. They were in the small town of Kelliher at that time. Ran a small hotel as I remember, and operated the town telephone system switch board right from their living room.

They later moved to the Minneapolis-St. Paul area for the more productive years of their lives, but it was back to Kelliher and the giant Red Lake and places like Bemidji in the home territory of the mythical lumberjack Paul Bunyon and his Babe-the-Blue-Ox land.

I'd love to visit them again and do some of the small-town things we did on that trip. Like crossing the beginnings of the great Mississippi River in one step, playing softball in the school yard with locals who had difficulty understanding Southern speech, but who laughed and fellowshipped and welcomed us like long-lost friends. I'd like to run the switchboard again, and visit in their friend's home even though they fed us tuna salad with green peas and macaroni in it!

Everywhere you go in Northern Minnesota, they feed you. From a snack to a full meal, you're expected to eat.

And the beauty of the countryside is literally breath-taking. We were there in summer, but I'd like to see it in the full-blown, white beauty of winter. For a few days that is. I hope they love their snow because I'm certainly not used to it and we don't want it down South. I'd like to just experience it—not live in it!

The husband of one of my cousins, a native Minnesotian, used to rag me about how slow the South was and how far we were behind in everything, including agriculture. He said that every farmer in Minnesota had a tractor, while most Southern farmers still used mules.

I didn't have much of a comeback for him at that early age, but things do tend to work out in the end. Minnesota still has something that South Carolina doesn't have, but it's called Jesse "The Body" Ventura! How 'bout that, Gov? Still think we're the ones who are behind?

OSHKOSH, WISCONSIN

By far the best time to be in Oshkosh, as far as I'm concerned, is around the last of July, first week of August when the Experimental Aircraft Association has their annual fly-in convention. This get-to-gather brings in aviation buffs from around the world—many of them flying their own airplanes.

According to the television coverage I've seen of this event, you'll find just about every kind of aircraft that's ever been built. From experimental single-seaters powered by a lawn mower engine (or slightly more), to the largest planes in the air (like the Concord and military transport planes.)

The old Warbirds from World Wars I and II fly side-by-side with sleek experimentals lovingly built in someone's garage. Airworthy airplanes and partial airplanes, spare parts for people who are restoring old models, the latest in aviation equipment and clothing, food by the ton and people by the hundreds of thousands—these are the staples in Oshkosh during that airborne-from-the ground-to-the-sky celebration.

My seatmate on a recent flight was an Oshkosh native. "Lots of us rent out parts, or all of our homes during that time," he said. "For those of us who love the airplanes and the celebration, it's a real battle with ourselves whether we want to stay and see the shows, or rent the house and bring in some big bucks."

NEW ENGLAND

Never been there, except through the courtesy of the library. Visited New York once when I was 17 and selected as the youngest disc jockey in the nation for a week-long announcer's duty on a national show on the Mutual Network, but that's a different story.

Didn't get to New England on that trip. I'm almost overcome when I see pictures of the rocky coastline, the small but filled-to-capacity fishing harbors, the lobster stands and restaurants with their New England boils and whole lobsters and clams, the quaint country roads and small towns and the beauty of the leaves in the fall.

I'd like to experience the history of Boston, the beauty of Booth Bay Harbor, the quaint rural villages of New Hampshire and Vermont. I'd like to hear the poetry of the land and the sea of Old Cape Cod and Martha's Vineyard. I'd like to listen to the people tell me what they love about their homeland.

I'd like to sail under full canvas, ride a lobster boat for a day, help mend a fishing net, build a wooden boat, collect sap from Maple trees and fire the boilers for making Maple syrup. Then I'd like to sample it.

SAN FRANCISCO

It would be great to find the little apartment on the side street in Alameda where Joyce and I first set up housekeeping. We'd retrace our route over the Bay Bridge from Oakland to San Francisco, marvel at the mid-point where it was anchored on Treasure Island and then on into the romance and adventure of San Francisco itself.

We'd look for the little German restaurant atop Knob Hill, ride the cable cars, eat fresh-boiled crabs on Fisherman's Wharf and look through the telescopes at the Golden Gate Bridge and Alcatraz.

We'd go north across the Golden Gate to Sausalito and marvel at the talent on display in this artist mecca. The characters living out their lives in full view of the tourists and the normal locals would never cease to delight us.

Once again we'd be in awe of the majestic Redwoods of the Muir Forest. We'd sit for hours on our way back and watch the seals cavorting on the rock-strewn beaches. Then we'd visit the Top of the Mark (Mark Hopkins Hotel) if it's still there.

We'd drive south on the coast highway, and though we'd never have to leave the road to take in our quota of beauty of sea and mountains, we would take such side trips as to the picture-postcard cities of Monterey and Pacific Grove.

SAN ANTONIO

We passed through San Antonio on our way back to South Carolina from California when the naval career came to an end. We'd visited Los Angeles, Hollywood, the Grand Canyon and a few other places by that time.

We really wanted to see the Alamo where fellow-South Carolinians had help defend the real estate and freedom from attacks by the Mexicans, but we couldn't find it. We were so tired that I don't remember how hard we really looked. Our next planned stop was New Orleans and perhaps we were a bit more interested in the Big Easy that we were in the Alamo.

If I ever get back, the Alamo will be my first stop, and the Riverwalk, home of the Jim Cullum Jazz band, will be my second stop. I listen to the band every Friday night on PBS Radio.

I'm sure there's a lot more interesting attractions in this Texas city, but the two listed are by far enough reason for a return visit.

Well, that's about enough of that. There are lots of other places I could add to the list like the Buffalo Bill Museum in Cody, Wyoming; the George Patton Museum in Ft. Knox, Kentucky; Niagara Falls; the Pennsylvania Dutch Country; the great Salt Lake, etc.

How about your list? You can check it out at the library.

Chapter 25

The Joy of Potato Chips

I was brought up on potato chips. Early in life, I came to the realization that a sandwich without potato chips was like a hot dog without chili, ice cream without a cone, apple pie without crust.

When I had to go on my rather severe diet later in life, potato chips were one of the first things I had to scratch off the list of favorite foods. That list got whittled down considerably, but I don't believe there was anything I missed more than those crunchy delights.

Even today, when I walk down the "chip" aisle in the grocery store, I have to close my eyes to avoid the temptation. I long for the good old days when I could tear open the pack and enjoy a trip to taste bud city for a short while, or as long as the bag lasted.

Remember that advertising slogan: "You can't eat just one!" I believe that is the truest advertising statement I've ever experienced. It certainly was in my case.

A Real Chip Aficionado

In order to qualify as a true addict, or lover, or buff, or devotee of the chip, it is my opinion that one has to develop more than just a craving for the salty, crispy, little potato wafer that literally seduces the taste buds. One has to know what one desires most from this true snack delight in order to be a chip gourmet. In other words, you have to expect more than just the taste.

I qualified because of a particular habitué for one distinctive shape of chip, of which there are only a few in each bag. Although I liked them all, it was my modus operandi to shake the bag gently and look first for the chips that were doubled over—not just a flat wafer shape, but ones that had folded themselves into a double shape during the frying process.

Sometimes when one is riding the crest of a fantastic wave of luck, you may even find two flat chips that have folded themselves together into a double-double and become one! Oh, joy!

Probably one of the finest moments of my eating career came on a summer afternoon when I was seated on the patio with a glass of lemonade and a bag of chips. Right there on top, when I ripped open the bag, was a THREE-CHIP-DOUBLE, perfectly folded, just waiting for me! Imagine—three chips folded together. Oh, triple joy!

In my excitement, I almost crushed the entire bag as my hands trembled, my arms twitched, sweat broke out on my forehead. I usually eat doubled chips first, but I gently lifted this one out of the bag, gave it a place of honor on my lap while I ate the rest of the bag. Then, while enjoying the breeze and the relaxation, I savored the thought of eating that triple-chip-double.

By saving it until last, I let it know how greatly I appreciated all its efforts in the bonding of the three chip buddies, giving me a true moment of happiness and pure enjoyment. Later after eating the most rare of chip delicacies, I lovingly folded that potato chip bag and tucked it away in the top drawer of my chest. For many months, every time I got out a clean pair of socks, I saw that bag and relived the excitement of finding the THREE-CHIP-DOUBLE.

Word From the Experts

While writing about my chip experience, I decided to call Frito-Lay—probably the best, or at least one of the best known names in Chipdom. The young woman in Customer Service, who answered the phone, quickly agreed with me that folded chips are the absolute best.

"What causes some to double over and most not to?" I asked, "and does Frito-Lay have a name for this phenomenon?"

She put me on hold to check with someone in the technical division of the company. After a couple of minutes, she was back.

"It has to do with the moisture content of the potato," she answered. "Some have more moisture than others, therefore only some of them fold over when they're cooked . . . and no, we don't have a particular name for that. We just call them folded or doubled over chips."

"Just so I can accurately inform my readers about this important matter," I continued, "did the technical expert say whether potatoes with more or less moisture are the ones that tend to fold?"

She didn't know that—she just knew that it had to do with the moisture content of the individual potato. But she did say that she liked them too. "We all think the doubled overs are the best!"

I thanked her and went back to the computer to finish this semi-exciting adventure. If someone from Frito-Lay ever reads this, I might suggest to them that they really investigate this true food marvel and determine whether it is potatoes with more, or with less moisture, that are the ones tending to fold over.

That way they could produce entire bags of doubled over chips and probably charge a lot more for them. They might even be able to duplicate the famous TRIPLE-DOUBLE of my treasured memories.

Chapter 26

Amish Cousins Know Country Cooking

I've always been partial to country cooking. Well, for that matter I've always been partial to almost any kind of cooking, but country is what I was brought up on and it has always remained number one.

There are lots of restaurants that serve up this wonderful, only-in-America food, but I want to tell you about two here in South Carolina that I think you'll rate as tops in your book. They are in mine.

Both are owned by Mennonites, both are family operations, both give you your dollars worth of fantastic country food that'll give your tummy a holiday of happiness. One of these restaurants is in the small town of Abbeville, the other is in the smaller town of Blackville.

In case you don't know a lot about the Mennonite religion, I'll tell you in the words of one of these restaurant owners. Mennonites might be described as first cousins to the Amish. Although Amish are generally regarded as much more conservative and strict in their ways of not giving in to modern conveniences and modes of transportation, Mennonites are divided between the more conservative and the little bit less conservative ways of life.

Amish or Mennonite, you'll probably never meet finer people or enjoy finer food than that which emanates from the Pennsylvania Dutch tradition of table fare.

Yoder's Dutch Kitchen

Henry and Verna Yoder didn't have any idea of owning a restaurant when they moved to Abbeville from Virginia, but someone told them this area really needed a good restaurant. In 1970 they opened to an enthusiastic crowd of excited local diners who have remained loyal through the years. It wasn't long after the opening, however, that the locals had to start sharing their new culinary treasure with visitors from across the state as word quickly spread about the fantastic food and even more fantastic deserts.

You'll find several types of meats available to go with the fresh vegetables and wonderful casseroles. Try the broccoli-rice casserole with the baked chicken livers (you'll have a hard time believing they aren't fried) and you'll make your stomach smile.

Homemade cornbread and rolls are high on the list of favorites. Then top off your meal with a desert, maybe something exotic like Shoo-fly pie, or something down-to-earth like chocolate peanut butter pie. Like apple fritters? You won't find better.

Another enjoyable aspect of dining in these restaurants is that you won't be rushed, and won't feel as though you should hurry through your meal . . . Take your time and enjoy the food. Everyone around you will be doing the same, so you'll feel right at home. Service is prompt and friendly, and the iced tea is delicious.

Yoder's is located on Highway 72. It is open for lunch on Wednesday and Thursday, lunch and dinner on Friday and Saturday.

If you're looking for a good excuse to drive to that part of the state, that is something other than just a great dining experience, plan a visit to the Park Seed Company in nearby Greenwood. Enjoy seeing this great flower and garden emporium that has a world-wide reputation, shop in their exciting garden shop and then drive the 12 miles or so on to Abbeville.

I can promise . . . you won't be disappointed.

Miller's Bread-Basket

Although not quite as fancy as Yoder's, the tiny town of Blackville is justifiably proud of its own Mennonite restaurant, Miller's Bread-Basket.

Ever been to a restaurant where you could buy a "half portion" of a main meat dish, or a half portion of vegetables? This feature at Miller's is especially appreciated by many senior citizens. Of course, for connoisseurs like you and me, "full" portions are also available!

There aren't many different ways to describe or explain country cooking, but those of us who appreciate it would much rather experience the taste than listen to the description.

Ray Miller is proud of the fact that they bake their own bread right there in the restaurant, and that "fresh" vegetables are featured in season every day. Casseroles are also big here. The usual selections of meats are not just "usually" prepared, they have a little special flair that makes them a bit more tasty than what you're probably used to.

If you have any room left after enjoying your selections from the serving bar, try one of the at least 10 desserts you'll find waiting for you.

After the meal, stroll from the restaurant to the other side of the building where you'll find an intriguing gift and antique shop

Miller's Bread-Basket is open for lunch on Monday, Wednesday and Saturday. On Tuesday, Thursday and Friday, take your choice of lunch or supper (dinner for those of you who prefer).

Abbeville or Blackville—take your choice for good country food. Better idea, try them both!

Chapter 27

All Pigs Ain't Pork Chops

By the time you make it all the way through these pages, you'll probably have deduced that food is, and always has been, one of my favorite pastimes. My discussion of culinary delights would not be complete without a dissertation on Bar-B-Que.

I've eaten it in Texas where I had beef, doused with ketchup, and called Bar-B-Que. I've eaten it in North Carolina where they use pork and spice it up with pepper-vinegar sauce. Now I'll have to admit that early I developed a liking for this particular concoction, and still have been known to look for some of this good eating every time I cross the Northern South Carolina border. You'll also find a few places in the Palmetto State that feature pepper-vinegar.

In South Carolina, you'll also find only pork (not beef) used (as is the case throughout most of the South), but you'll find two distinctive kinds of sauce—mustard based and tomato (or ketchup) based. Let me add here that chicken is also a favorite when it is cooked over the coals and doused with healthy applications of the appropriate liquid.

When I first came to the Columbia area, I didn't really know what to expect. I'd heard people in the Lowcountry who survived on tomato-based Bar-B-Que say that up in the Midlands they boiled pork, poured mustard on it and called it Bar-B-Que.

Since I've been in the Midlands for so long, and since that's about the only kind of pig pickings' available, I've kinda grown accustomed to mustard-based. But I still like that pepper-vinegar every chance I get.

Liven Up A Turkey

My Lowcountry cousin would delight the family at Thanksgiving celebrations by bringing a Bar-B-Qued turkey. The gentleman who specialized in these, and from whom she bought, would split the turkey at the breast and then lay it out on a huge grill.

He used a pepper-vinegar sauce that was spicy enough to add a bit of zing to the bird. I've tried to find someone in this area of the state who uses this method for a holiday turkey, but with no luck.

Everyone I've heard about who prepares turkeys for sale offers deep fried ones, but no grilled-over-coals gobblers.

If you ever get a chance to try Bar-B-Qued turkey with this type of sauce, don't pass up the opportunity. It's delicious. Goes well with dressing, baked sweet potatoes, sweet potato soufflé, rice and gravy, green beans and all those other holiday accouterments.

For you tailgaters, your guests would probably go wild over this offering if you could find one, or perhaps fix one yourself.

Favorite Eateries

I've got to admit that I find it hard to pass by any place that has a Bar-B-Que shingle hanging out front, and I've found great pork and trimmings at lots of places in the Palmetto State, but my family has kinda narrowed our enjoyment of this Southern delicacy to three places.

(I realize I've written out Bar-B-Que quite a few times already. Some of you would probably shorten this to read Bar-B-Q. With your consent, from now on, I'll simply refer to the subject at hand as B-B-Q).

Shealy's

I guess this has to be the B-B-Q capitol of the world. If you've never been to this grand emporium of pork and chicken in Leesville, you're a member of a very small minority in the region. You owe yourself a visit so you can convince your taste buds for once that they've really served their purpose.

While the mustard-based B-B-Q and hash are probably the top drawing card, this serve-yourself and eat-all-you-want restaurant also has some of the best fried chicken that'll ever cross your lips. The fried chicken livers are out of this world, and for you fried gizzard lovers—you'll not be disappointed either.

In addition you'll find greens, great green beans (one of the restaurant's favorite dishes),cream-style corn, sweet potatoes, slaw, potato salad, macaroni and cheese, cornbread, banana pudding, soft ice cream and a full-service salad bar among other things.

Another recommendation, and this goes for practically every B-B-Q place I've ever eaten—the iced tea is outstanding. I don't know what it is about this beverage, but nothing goes better with a fine Southern meal like this than iced tea. Perhaps there's something in the cooking of the pork and/or chicken that compliments good, sweet, cold, tea.

Don't be bashful at Shealy's. Try everything that strikes your fancy, but they do hate to see you leave food on your plate. Like I tell the grandchildren, if you're new to a buffet and see lots of items you'd like to try, take small portions. You can always go back for more when you discover a winner.

By the way, if you love ribs, Monday is your day for a visit to Shealy's. On Tuesday you'll find catfish stew. Don't do as I did and drive over on Wednesday, dreaming of a great mid-week meal. Found out when I got there, they're closed on Wednesdays. 'Twas a sad drive back to Columbia. I was pretty hungry, but when you're set for dining at Shealy's, no place else seems right. You'll find they also take the day off on Sundays.

Millender's

Located on the I-26 frontage road at the intersection of Highway 378 near the Lexington Medical Center in West Columbia, Millender's is tucked away in a quiet corner.

You may walk in the door as a stranger, but you'll quickly find that as good as the food are the friendly folks who keep the vitals coming and the buffet full. Lots of family involved here, and they'll treat you just like kin.

The hash is one of my favorites at Millender's, but then so are the B-B-Q and the ribs. I like the ones that don't have a lot of meat on the bone, but often I have to really look to find any like this. Most of them are really thick and tender.

The B-B-Q has mustard-based sauce, but the ribs don't. Of course, there's always plenty in containers on the tables if you want to add some.

You'll also find fried and B-B-Q chicken to go with the green beans, sweet potatoes, slaw, corn, pork and beans, greens, French fries, hush puppies and the salad bar, complete with potato salad.

Yes, they do have light bread. Most restaurants of this type have to have loaves of the sliced bread out for customers. The last time at Millender's, I pointed out one man at a table near us who had a stack of light bread atop his pile of B-B-Q and other goodies.

"That man's got six slices of light bread," I told the members of my family at our table. "If he sat down with six slices, he must have eaten two on the way to his table," my daughter countered. "When he passed by us he had eight!"

When you finish off your plate, hope you've left room for some Banana Pudding. Unlike some of the bananaless pudding I've eaten at other places, Millender's uses bananas and real Vanilla Wafers!

Millender's is open Thursdays, Fridays and Saturdays. A special treat for you fish lovers, on Thursday nights you'll also find fried catfish, catfish nuggets, flounder filets, grits, stewed tomatoes and catfish stew in addition to the regular B-B-Q offerings.

Same price! No extra charge for the fish. Eat all you want.

Bobby's

Let's face it, most of the food you'll find at B-B-Q restaurants has a pretty high fat content. Lots of times even most of the vegetables dishes are pretty solidly seasoned with fat back (sometimes streak-o-lean). But these are not the places to go if you're looking for a low-fat diet.

I say this, but was I in for an unbelievable pleasant surprise the first time I visited Bobby's B-B-Q on U.S. Highway One between Aiken and Augusta (about six miles out of Aiken). They feature a low-fat (or no-fat) dish and guess what it is—BAR-B-QUE!

Well, at least one of their B-B-Q offering is minus the fat—the other kind is not! Couldn't wait to try this gastronomic oxymoron—no fat B-B-Q.

Owner Bobby Griffin told me that they leave the fat out of this chipped up pork and don't use a sauce on it. They do baste it with pepper and vinegar. I didn't know it, but he said the vinegar also helps lower the cholesterol content of the meat.

Now I'm not going to sit here and tell you that this no-fat B-B-Q will satisfy your cravings for good, ole', fat-laced B-B-Q, but it sure comes in a close second. I guess what made it so appealing to me was that I could eat it without a feeling of guilt starting at my tongue and working itself all the way down!

I really don't know how much good it'll do you to put a helping of no-fat B-B-Q in a corner, and then load the rest of the plate up with hash (it's delicious) and rice, hush puppies, chicken and all the other good stuff that you'll find in this scrupulously clean, log cabin-looking restaurant.

And least you think your B-B-Q taste buds will be cheated because there's only no-fat B-B-Q, let me quickly ease your mind. You'll also find something on the buffet line that looks like regular B-B-Q you've seen at other restaurants—it does include fat.

But once again, Bobby offers you a real surprise. He calls the other variety—Pulled B-B-Q. He explained that the three varieties that most people are familiar with are: mustard based, tomato based and pepper-vinegar based sauce, as we've discussed earlier.

His Pulled version has a sauce that is made up of—you guessed it—mustard, tomato, pepper and vinegar. There you go B-B-Q lovers—he's got all the bases covered at the same time!

I defy you to go into Bobby's and not find something or some things that will make your stomach smile. Can't be done.

And before I forget, if you like ribs you've found the end of your gastronomic rainbow! They're BIG with a capital B I G. I said earlier that I like the kind of ribs with a bone that don't have a lot of meat on them. I do not go by this rule at Bobby's.

You can't go by this rule at Bobby's—the ribs are heafty. Again, they don't have sauce on them, but you can add all you want. It comes in mild and hot, and the hot will leave you with something to remember on your trip home.

Well, there you've got my three choices. Like I said, there are many, many more B-B-Q restaurants of fine repute from border to border—from shining sea to towering mountains in the Palmetto State. Places like Dukes, and Schoolhouse, and Brown's and Sikes', and Hite's, and Little Pigs, and Piggie Park—I enjoy them all!

What a shame . . . so many good places to eat real Bar-B-Que and only seven days in a week.

(Editor's Note—All of these restaurants are closed on certain days. Make a phone call before you travel long distances to try the great food. That way you won't be disappointed by finding the restaurant dark.)

Chapter 28

Did You Ever Wonder Why:

• A steak that costs enough to break your food budget can be that tough?

• Grocery store plastic bags, which have practically replaced paper, seem to have handles that give way mostly when the bag is filled with eggs, or with things in glass bottles that will break when they hit the pavement?

• Something that smells as bad as collards when they are cooking are good to eat? And something that smells as good as honeysuckle in the wild isn't?

• Even with a full congregation at the service, the preacher's remarks so often seem to be directed straight at you? And to make matters even worse, they're right on the mark

• Television news really isn't news any more? It's more what newspapers call editorial pages. With a slight twist of the mouth, cocking of the head, raising of the eyebrows, shrugging of the shoulders, frown, laugh or the way they read the copy, TV anchors and reporters put their own influence or twist on just about every piece they do.

• The fish always bite the day before you go fishing, or the day after you go?

• Gasoline prices always go up just before a major holiday, whether there's a surplus of gas or a shortfall?

• When your children need a doctor, it's usually after midnight or on a weekend?

• Even though we're not in an inflationary period, prices at the grocery store keep going higher while prices the farmer gets for his products keep going lower?

• When you take your car in for one of those cheap oil changes, they often find something wrong with the vehicle that will set you back more bucks than you thought you were going to save by taking advantage of that advertised special?

• You always get in the wrong line at the bank or the check-out counter? You think you're the only one? Wrong, I'm usually in that same line—right behind you!

• The doctor schedules three or four other people at the same time as your appointment? And why you're usually the last one booked for that period they call back to an examining room? And then the doctor has to leave the room to go take a call from another doctor that he's been waiting for all day.

• The people seated at the table next to you in a restaurant always have some medical problem they need to discuss while you're trying to eat?

• If there's a crying or unruly child in the restaurant, he/she will be seated at the table next to yours?

Chapter 29

More Than Just Bad Luck!

One night recently, as I began to clean up the kitchen and wash the dishes, the usual aggravation with the kitchen sink almost ruined what had been a pretty nice day. While l was rinsing off some dishes to put in the dishwasher, the strainer basket in the sink wouldn't stay in the open position. Instead of letting the water drain down the standpipe, the sink kept filling up. I had to re-set it several times.

Then, when I wanted to fill the sink with water to wash the pots and pans, the strainer basket wouldn't stay in the closed position. My dishwater kept draining out.

Occurrences such as these are the story of my life. If I'm using the vacuum cleaner, the cord keeps hanging up on a piece of furniture. When I pull to try to free it, the vacuum tips over. If I want a door to stay open, it always closes. If I want it to close, it remains open.

I inevitable pick the wrong line at the bank, grocery store, ticket office, fast food palace, Highway Department license office or anywhere else there is a choice.

The World's Most Evil Stoplight

Here's one I've been fighting for 40 years. When I leave my driveway and head for the stoplight a couple of blocks away—a stoplight at an intersection where traffic enters from five directions—I know when I pull up to that light it will be changing from green to red, or have just have changed. When I look across the intersection and see that line of cars just starting to move, I know I've hit that intersection at the longest possible cycle that light goes through. I'll be sitting there staring at that red light for well more than two or three minutes.

This doesn't just happen occasionally. I've actually kept records for part of the 40 years I've been living in this house. Those documents show that about 99.5 percent of the time, I catch that light as

I've described. I've actually sat in the car in the driveway with the motor running for up to a minute, to see if this would change my luck. Then I'd back out into the street and head for the intersection. Sure enough, as I round the slight curve just before the light, it'll change, or it'll be red and I look across to find that other row of cars just starting to move.

I've driven those two blocks very fast, or extremely slow to see if that has any effect on my catching that light green. It doesn't. I'll bet I can count on two hands the number of times I've caught that light green in the last 40 years.

Applies Even to Shopping and Dog Racing

If I buy an appliance, a piece of electronics, a power saw, a flashlight from a stack of 20 to 25 boxes, I'll pick one that doesn't work. The last can of spray paint I bought didn't even have one of those plastic buttons you mash to let the paint come out.

Got a pack of emergency candles. Opened them up one dark night and the wicks weren't sticking out the end of the candles so you could light them.

Bet on a dog at the dog racing track in Miami, Florida, one night after having picked three winners in a row in earlier races without placing a bet. The dog I bet on didn't even come out of the starting box! Track attendants had to go out and kick the box to make the dog come out after the race was over.

When I was commissioned in the Navy, I asked for a small ship in the Atlantic and they put me on the world's largest ship—an aircraft carrier in the Pacific.

There're a lot more similar type happenings, but I think you get the idea To sum it up, I told my wife one day: "This has to be more than just bad luck. Something, somebody, some scheme has got to be behind this, or at least be involved in it. I can't figure it out."

Thanks Charles Kuralt

I walk for an hour every day with my portable radio and headphones to keep me company. During hot summer weather, or cold winter weather, I walk at the mall. Because of all the steel in the structure, it is hard to listen to my favorite radio stations, so I started listening to audio tapes to help make the hour pass faster.

I checked out a set of tapes by the late Charles Kuralt, the famous CBS Correspondent of *ON THE ROAD* and *SUNDAY MORNING* fame. Kuralt had always been one of my favorite writers and broadcasters. When he died on July 4, 1997, I felt a particular loss although I'd never met the man.

A couple of people have told me that pieces I've done reminded them of the way Kuralt wrote. I don't know whether or not they realized it, but those were the best compliments I think I've ever gotten.

The tape I was listening to this time was a recording Kuralt had made reading his book, *CHARLES KURALT'S AMERICA*.

Could This Be The Answer?

As I turned the corner at Chic-Fil-A and headed on the long shopping straight-away, Kuralt really caught my attention. He was interviewing a local long-time resident of Ely, Minnesota, during his visit there for a chapter in the book. They were talking about the Ojibwa Indians, who were described as good, honest people . . .

He told Kuralt about a special way the members of this tribe had of dealing with adversity. Rather than blame little accidents like losing an item, or falling down, or spilling something on themselves or another member of the tribe, they'd shrug and laugh and say it was the Little People, whom they called the Maymayguishi, who caused the problem.

He said they believed the Little People loved to cause mischief, play tricks on others to make them mad. They lived in the spirit lakes and he said sometimes you could hear them laughing in the tops of the trees.

Could this possibly be what has caused my troubles and tribulations all these years? RIGHT! Remember that time I had traveled to northern Minnesota when I was in high school. Went up there with my Aunt and Uncle to visit some other relatives.

I went in the woods a lot while I was there, went fishing several times on one of Minnesota's 10,000 lakes. I'll bet those Little People lived in the waters of that lake—Red Lake I believe the name was! I'll bet they were in the tops of those trees in the woods where we played. Seems I definitely remember my life had been pretty good,

115

pretty uneventful up until that point. It was later that these "unusual" things started happening.

The more I think about it, there seems to be little doubt about the cause of my problems. Some of those Little People latched onto me during my visit and followed me home to South Carolina. Probably even followed me when I went into the Navy. They've evidently been around ever since, playing tricks on me, making me get mad, making things happen like that evil stoplight. Unfortunately I had never heard of the Ojibwa Indians until I was listening to this tape walking in the mall. Before this tape, I didn't know who or what was the cause of all my trials and tribulations.

Trying Hard

For the last week or so, I've been trying very hard not to lose my temper and blame myself when the dumpster door closes on my finger, or the cord of my portable radio gets caught on the door knob and pulls the earphones off my head as I'm leaving to go walking. Or when I see the lady at Chic-Fil-A putting away the platter and cutting board where she's been handing out delicious samples just as I round the corner all cocked and prime for a tasty morsel to help the walk go faster. She closes up every day promptly at 2 o'clock, you see.

Oh well, don't blame yourself, now I say. It was the Little People who wrapped the headphone cord around the door knob, and who made you late at the mall today so you missed a sample piece of chicken. You'll have to wait 'till tomorrow for a handout.

They also probably sneaked around and put weak batteries in my radio—the sound seems to be trailing off again. Better change them when I get home, and I'll be sure to throw the old batteries away before the Little People get hold of them and trick somebody else.

I'm almost positive now when I leave home and find that light at the intersection red, that I can hear the Little People laughing in the tops of the trees in the adjoining church yard.

Thanks, Charles. I'm so happy you did that piece. Like I told my wife, there had to be an answer. I knew all along it was more than just bad luck!

(A Postscript—I have always been a fan of Charles Kuralt, and enjoyed everything he ever wrote, but in this book *CHARLES KURALT'S AMERICA*, I find him at his best. Published in 1995 by G.P. Putnam's Sons, it was written after he retired from CBS. He took a year off and revisited 12 places in America that, over the years, had become his favorites. He spent a month in each location, mostly just visiting or hanging out. Then he wrote about the things he did during that month. My home state, South Carolina, was on his list of 12—Charleston being the location he chose. I highly recommend this book. If you're too busy to read it, or if you grew so accustomed to his voice on television that you'd rather hear him read it, then listen to the audio version he recorded. I did both.)

Chapter 30

Sippin' Pot Liquor, Eatin' Rice Cake

You may not want to admit it, but if you were brought up in a small town or in the country in the South, you probably know exactly what I'm talking about.

Rice cake was my favorite. No, it's not a desert. If you've ever cooked rice in a non, non-stick pot, chances are the bottom got a bit overdone. Some stuck to the pot and turned kinda brown and crispy. This is rice cake.

One of my favorites was when Mother cooked chicken bog, or chicken pilau as we called it. We pronounced pilau (purr-low). She'd boil the chicken, cook rice in the broth that resulted, then take the chicken off the bone and stir it up with the rice. She was a great cook—never knew her to burn anything, but she'd always overcook that rice a bit because she knew how much I loved what came out of the bottom of the pot. Rice cake from squirrel pilau was also good, but the chicken was better.

But my all-time favorite was Red Rice rice cake. Georgetown (or Charleston—they're very similar) Red Rice is rice cooked in stewed tomatoes and bacon drippings. The last meal she cooked for me before her death was Red Rice, baked chicken and broccoli. At the bottom of that pot was the best rice cake I've ever tasted— cooked just to the point of being as crisp as fried bacon.

Pot Liquor Ain't Distilled

I'll have to admit I never cared much for this delicacy, but among some country folks it went over pretty big. For you uninitiated, pot liquor is the liquid left over after you get through cooking veg-etables—namely greens (collard, mustard, turnip,) or even peas and beans.

We have one friend from Summerton (you can't get much more Southern than that) who is as big on pot liquor as I am on rice cake. I've seen him hoist a pot to his lips, (after the greens were taken up for serving) much the same as the old timers would hoist a jug of 'White Lightnin', and not sit it down 'till he'd drained the last drop.

Weird Taste Sensations

My children used to be amazed, and at times a bit horrified, at some of the taste combinations I favored. Loved banana sandwiches with mayonnaise on one slice of bread and peanut butter on the other. I also like to spread pimento cheese on cookies; put peanut butter on apples, pears and pretzels; eat Oreo cookies with vegetable soup; combine salted peanuts with chocolate cake; potato chips with lemon or chocolate meringue pie.

There are also some things that are just as good to me cold as they are hot. These include: cooked cabbage, spaghetti with meat sauce, garden peas and Brussels sprouts.

I'll admit that some of these might be strange to you, but you really shouldn't knock it unless you've at least tried it.

Grandchildren Follow in Step

My grandchildren have evidently inherited a few genes which are allowing them to follow Granddaddy's taste traditions. You see, I think I inherited some of this from my Daddy. The dish he favored over all others was to crumble up cornbread in clabber. If there was no clabber available, he'd accept buttermilk. If there was no cornbread available, he'd settle for biscuits.

But back to the grandchildren. They've even come up with some doozies of their own—completely different and foreign to mine.

Rachael, the oldest, is probably the most fanatical rice aficionado I've ever seen. Mostly she likes it plain, although she is also partial to Chinese shrimp fried rice and to her Mother's chicken bog. But her all-time favorite was discovered at Millender's Bar-B-Que restaurant in West Columbia.

She loves the dill chip pickles they serve. She loves the rice they serve. Therefore, she loves to fill up a salad bowl with rice and then soak this with dill chip pickles and pickle juice! How's that for originality?

Allison, the youngest, also has a curious combination that she developed at Millender's. She likes to put the liver hash on rice and then put this in a piece of lightbread, folding it to make her own special sandwich. That make you lick your lips in anticipation?

Courtney, the middle granddaughter, is probably the green bean queen, at least of central South Carolina. She's been known to go to a "meat and three vegetables" restaurant and order three servings of green beans to go with the meat course.

Even my next-door-neighbor dog, Dusty, gets into the act. He just loves Coca-Cola and Granny Smith Apples. He also likes to finish up the last bit of coffee from my mug.

I'll bet you have some favorite taste combinations of your own, but unlike my family, you may be too sensitive to mention yours. Bet you enjoy them just the same though, don't you? Even if you'd have to admit that people may think you weird for putting ketchup (or catsup or catchup) on your scrambled eggs or chocolate syrup on your hush puppies.

Chapter 31

Hide the Tools

Mechanical ability! What a wonderful blessing to be able to work with your hands, to build things, take broken things apart, put them back together and see them work again. Some people can accomplish miracles, others can work wonders and some are only semi-successful.

It's different with different people, but everyone has a certain degree of manual dexterity. Want to bet?

The Navy decided to test my mechanical aptitude to help determine into which slot I would best fit. They couldn't even score the test! "Look, Chief," I said trying to help ease his frustration, "in order to test for something, there has to be something there. Right?"

How many times have you heard mothers talk about their children: "He loves to take his toys apart and put them back together. He's a whiz at it."

My Mother used to confess to people: "Larry loves to take things apart, but he can never figure out how to put them back together. Once he takes them apart, that's it—never works again."

As I journeyed through life, I decided to become a writer, a wordsmith. Words have been my friends. They have mostly taken the place of my desire to build bridges and tall buildings. My backyard pirate ship satisfied my desire to be the world's best boat builder.

Friends as I am with the language, there are three words that have continually pierced my heart with fear and brought temporary paralysis to my brain: SOME ASSEMBLY REQUIRED! I quickly learned that many packagers at manufacturing plants must practice their weird sense of humor by including at least one extra screw, or by leaving out one necessary screw in every box. Never have I found the correct amount of screws to match the number of screw holes.

Young Ones Find Answer

My children figured it out best. "Daddy, why don't you ask Santa to put our toys together before he leaves the house?" they would suggest.

Even when they were small and something broke in our home or in our car, before they would tell me it was broken, they would hide my tools. "Daddy, call somebody to come fix it," they'd urge.

Although I persist to this day in trying to use a tool or two every now and then, I'm well aware of my lack of ability. But still I try. Sometimes I have semi-success, but only after making several attempts. I don't ever recall being successful on the first try. I always have to do it wrong a time or two before I see the light (dim as it is).

An Example

My wife had a 1979 Pontiac which we bought new. It was a doozie, but after some years the heater fan went bad.

"You can fix that in a jiffy," my mechanical-oriented neighbor announced. "All you've got to do is pull the old one out and stick a new one in."

First of all, I have determined that half of any successful car repair can be attributed to having the right tools. My rubber-coated-handle-pliers, a regular screw driver and a Phillips head screw driver were at the ready.

The second factor that determines whether or not you can fix what is wrong with an automobile is knowing what you can yank on, and what you can't yank on. You see, even when you succeed in unscrewing all the screws, unbolting all the bolts—nothing comes off or out easily. You usually either have to yank on it, or hammer on it or pry it off.

I always select the wrong piece to yank on, or hammer on or pry on. Most often it comes off in two pieces instead of one. There are not supposed to be two pieces.

To make a long story short, I took that bad heater fan out on the third attempt. Then I put the new heater fan in a total of 11 times before I got it right. Today I am an expert in how to, and how not to, replace the heater fan in a 1979 Pontiac LeMans. Only problem is we no longer have a 1979 Pontiac LeMans. Somebody else probably has it, Their heater fan probably still works so good they don't want to get rid of the car. I can just hear the new owner saying: "boy, somebody sure did a job on that heater fan!"

I'll Tell You How

While I am fully aware of my mechanical inaptitude, I do possess what I consider to be a considerable ability. I can tell you how to do what I can't. That's right, just take my advice and you won't go wrong.

I don't know how many articles I've written, after interviewing experts, to describe projects and how to construct them, equipment failures and how to fix them, furniture and how to build it, even houses and how to . . .

I think you get the idea.

I've had people tell me how wonderfully clear those articles were and what great success they had after following the instructions. I've let the compliments go to my head a few times to the point where I actually believed that anyone could take my article and successfully complete the described activity. I even believed that perhaps I could possibly follow my own instructions.

Guess what? Somebody should have hidden the tools again.

Chapter 32

Law of the Airplane

I've always loved airplanes. Just being around them gives me a great sense of adventure. There seems to be something magical about people who are pilots. They even appear to float a few feet above the ground when they are walking.

In my last job before retiring, I had to fly several times a year. With the uncertainty of schedules, lost luggage, crowded airports, narrow aisles and even narrower seats, it got to the point where flying wasn't fun anymore.

Some people will tell you they are more comfortable flying in big airplanes and they wouldn't dare get into a small plane. I always felt just the opposite. I love the adventure of the light aircraft. Always felt safe with the pilots I flew with. An airliner won't glide. When the engine cuts out, that's it. A light plane will glide for miles while you search for a safe spot in which to touch down if the engine quits.

I took my first airplane ride when I was in college, my second when I was in the Navy. After the "real" adventure of these first two flights, every other one really seemed tame. I've been on airliners with some "white knuckle" passengers. They'd grab those armrest and hang on for dear life—even when the plane was flying straight and level.

Let me tell you about my first two flights. In college, I had a summer intern job with the *Florence Morning News*. The local Civil Air Patrol unit was at an encampment in Greenville and I was assigned to do an article on them. They offered to send a plane to Florence to take me to the upstate.

I was waiting on the tarmac when a twin engine plane landed and taxied up to me. A Major open the door and motioned for me to climb aboard. He was the entire crew, and appeared to be in a hurry. Once I was in, he taxied out to the runway and revved up the engines.

As the plane was hurtling down the runway, he announced: "I've got a job for you."

"Sure," I quickly agreed.

"Keep your eye on that right engine for me. That *+#*=#D^8*&+* thing's been smoking all the way down here!" He let out a few more expletives, chomped down with a death grip on the stump of a cigar, and didn't say another word.

I looked down and all I could see was the concrete ribbon quickly falling away beneath us. That flight to Greenville seemed to take an eternity, and was none too enjoyable. But I kept a watch on the engine, and we did make it to our destination.

When we landed, he quickly taxied into a hangar and called over a mechanic. They took off the cowling from the right engine and immediately started cursing. The pilot looked at me.

"Every bit of insulation on every wire in that engine is burned away," he announced. "No way I'm going to be able to fly you back to Florence in this bucket of bolts when you get done with your story. Guess we'll have to take you back in one of the trucks."

That was the most promising statement I'd heard in the last few hours. The ride home took considerably longer, but I was much more at ease!

My second flight came when a buddy on my ship, the aircraft carrier USS Ranger, invited me to make the mail run with him. We were several hundred miles off the coast of South America on an extended cruise, and he made periodic trips to pick up our mail at points along our route.

After you take of with a catapult shot from a carrier, and then land on that pitching deck several hours later where your tail hook picks up one of the cables stretched across the flight deck and you go from 120 knots to dead still in the space of a few yards—even a rough flight on a major airliner is like a walk in the park.

Long after the Navy, when I owned a photography studio, I did quite a bit of aerial photography. For those of you who aren't familiar with commercial aerial photography, you put an awful lot of faith in your seat belt. Leaning out the side of a Piper Cub with the door removed to give you a better look, you have to have a good feeling about that belt and the pilot. Fortunately for me, that faith always proved to be justified.

More Flying Tales

An acquaintance of mine was employed by one of the major airlines. He used to tell some wild flying stories about his, and some of his co-worker's adventures. My job called for me to spend quite a few hours in the air, as well, en route to various meetings around the country. Believe me, you can hear of, and experience, some unusual airplane adventures—not only in the air but in airports as well.

I'll start off by telling you a couple of tales about a Southern lass who left home and moved up to the North country. She just had to come back South ever so often to visit and load up on good, Southern food to take home. Once she carried a container of collards on the airplane. Those of you familiar with the aroma of these fine greens can probably imagine the rest of the story.

Shortly after takeoff, her seatmates started sniffing, turning their nose from side to side, up and down, like a fine 'ole Black and Tan hound trying to pick up a trail. Pretty soon the entire passenger compartment was filled with the smell of collards. Everyone was sniffing but they couldn't figure out what the aroma was that filled the air, or where it was coming from.

She played along with the other passengers as she sniffed and waved her hand in front of her face as if trying to wipe away the stench. "I can't imagine what could smell like that," she announced to those around her. "Where could it be coming from?"

She was glad when the plane finally landed, her cargo undiscovered. She clutched the collards close to her as she deplaned and headed home with her treasure—people sniffing all along the way.

Pardon, Is That Your Hair?

Another time, she boarded a plane carrying an umbrella under her arm, plus a bag or two to go in the overhead bin. The aisle was crowded as usual. All of a sudden she was brought to an immediate standstill. She tried to move forward with no success. It seemed that her bag or something was hung up.

She strained to keep moving but she couldn't make any progress. Then she discovered the handle of her umbrella was the culprit. She pulled on it a couple of times. It gave a little. She heard a moan. Finally she was able to turn around. There, behind her, was a little old woman, stooped over and stumbling behind her down the aisle.

On closer examination, she discovered that the curved handle of her umbrella was caught in the wig the little woman was wearing. She was clawing at her head trying to untether herself from whatever it was that had entwined itself in her artificial hair. The wig evidently fit pretty tight, because she had been yanked completely out of her seat and a couple of rows down the aisle by the perky Southern lass.

I guess you had to be there to get the full impact.

Night Questions

Working the night shift apparently can provide some exciting phone calls, according to airline employees.

Answering the phone, one agent was hit with this question: "Mr. Airplane Man, what's the law of the airplane?

"What you mean, child?" he responded.

"You know, the law of the airplane. Like the law of the automobile is that when the light red, the car stops. When the light green, it go. How about the airplane?"

"Oh . . . I see. Well, the law of the airplane is that it has a red light on the end of one wing and a green light on the end of the other wing . . . " He paused for effect.

"So long as the pilot keep the airplane 'tween them two lights—EVERYTHING COOL."

Chapter 33

Why Doesn't Cucumber Start With a "Q"?

Did you ever try to explain to a four-year-old who has learned her alphabet, and who takes great joy in discovering which letter certain words begin with, why "cucumber" doesn't start with a "Q"?

If cat begins with a "C," then cucumber has to begin with a "Q." Explaining this to someone who doesn't give a rip about phonics is not the easiest exercise. But it is fun watching them learn—until they start getting into the bad habits!

Did you ever really stop to think about the educational process children go through? Did you ever stop to think about how they learn to tell lies or half truths, how they learn to criticize or play on our sympathy?

The answer is simple. They learn bad things the same way they learn good things—by example. They're supposed to understand that it is all right for us to tell the boss we're sick when we're not, but we sure did need a day at home away from the office. They're supposed to know it's really all right to tell the preacher we missed church because we were out of town on a business trip Sunday when they know you only went to the river to go fishing. But it's not all right for them to tell us they only ate one candy bar when they really had two.

We wonder why it seems so easy for our children to be taken in by the drug culture and to get hooked on those terrible destructive forces when all we do is have a social drink six or seven times a week, and maybe smoke a pack or two of cigarettes per day.

Did you ever notice how annoying it is when young ones are cross or go around whining or pouting about something that didn't go their way? Wonder where they picked up that irritating habit? Certainly your coming home from work in a complete uproar about office politics, and how you got chewed out for something that really wasn't your fault, didn't have anything to do with the child emulating that same type behavior.

Why are children often so hardheaded or stubborn? Can't imagine where they picked up these traits can we?

I guess the most amazing thing of all in watching the young ones learn is my own self discovery of how much wiser I've gotten on parental-type matters in later years—the same as I discovered how wise my parents were the older I became. Watching your grandchildren grow up is a bit easier in one way than when you watched your own children because you've gained from all the mistakes you made with your own. But some questions are still hard to answer, some values still hard to impart.

In the meantime, I'll continue to search for answers to try to help my grandchildren with their quest for knowledge—like why doesn't cucumber start with a "Q." I must confess that the more this subject is discussed, the more plausible it seems. I think I'm about to become a convert.

In fact, this spring I think I'm going to plant two rows of qcumbers.

Chapter 34

Take One...They're Free

I remember reading some years ago about a woman who was driving through a rural area with her husband who was on a business trip. They stopped at a small combination grocery store-gas station. She had to visit the restroom and this visit turned out to be one of the highlights of her trip.

Instead of finding a dirty, paper-strewn floor, graffiti covered walls and unkempt toilet, she was greeted by a tidy, clean but not beautiful, restroom. This was just the kind of discovery to raise the spirits of a weary traveler.

But what really caught her by surprise was a bright, shiny tin can, the paper label removed, filled to capacity with beautiful, freshly cut flowers. There was a small, pencil lettered sign resting against the can: Take one . . . they're free. She did so and walked back to the car with a smile on her face.

Every time I stop at a restroom on the road, usually disappointed at the filthy conditions I find, I remember this story and discover again why this experience meant so much to the traveler that she would take the time to write about it.

Little kindnesses can be bigger than we would ever realize, can mean more to strangers than we can imagine.

The Reverse Setting

I was walking through the mall the other day on my daily exercise excursion when I was taken aback by a sign in front of the florist shop. "What a turnaround," I said to myself, almost aloud, as the story of the flowers in the restroom came racing forward in my mind.

There on the flower cart outside the door, right next to some individually-wrapped, beautiful roses, was one of those little plastic storage bins—the kind that has the big, open squares so you can see what's inside. It was filled to capacity with copies of *Our Daily Bread*, a spiritually uplifting little publication which contains daily devotions for a time frame of three months.

Propped up against the carton was a little pencil-lettered sign that read: Take one . . . they're free!

First, flowers in the restroom . . . now, devotions in the florist shop. It gives you a good feeling to know that there are still people in the world who care . . . who care not only about themselves and their families, but even about strangers.

Is This Sign Following Me?

I visited the doctor's office last week, and as I stood at the window to pay for my visit and schedule my next appointment, there was a small table right next to the window. On it was a bright, multi-colored box, obviously professional designed and prepared to attract attention. It had a computer-generated sign: Take one . . . they're free.

The box contained envelopes, each with a two-day supply of a fiber laxative.

As I walked out to my car, I had to chuckle as I fondled the envelop I had picked up out of the box and read all about this product. Wouldn't it have been different, and uplifting, if that table had contained a bright, shiny tin can with label removed, filled to capacity with beautiful, freshly cut flowers, and a little pencil-lettered sign that said: Take one in good health . . . they're free?

Chapter 35

Me, a Gourmet? I Think Not...
(Or Why Skinny Gourmets Sometimes Get Sauced)

I like great food. I like good food. I've even been known to enjoy average food, and sometimes maybe even a bit-below-standard fare. But a gourmet I'm not. Probably a meat-potato-vegetable-man would be a better description.

I've eaten in quite a few fancy restaurants in lots of big cities, mostly when on business travel. All too often, I've found that gourmet dishes mean you get extra small servings at extra high prices.

Once, the vegetable portion of my meal consisted of three rather long string beans that had been slightly warmed—not cooked. Another time, my plate held two very small, asparagus spears.

Then on another occasion, there were four small cubes of yellow, summer squash mixed with several slithers of onion and a few bits of stewed tomatoes. Broiled tomatoes were on another gourmet platter. There were one and a half tiny cherry tomatoes, sliced, with some kind of sauce dabbed on the top of two of the pieces and put in the broiler for a minute or two.

Your plate may contain potatoes of some type, but they won't be called just potatoes. Gourmet cooks like exotic names. In one restaurant, my selection included "pomme de terr" with some kind of exotic name I couldn't come close to pronouncing. When the plate came, I discovered they were boiled potatoes with a bit of butter and some green sprinkles on them. I've also seen these billed as Florida Keys Potatoes.

Pilaf is another favorite of gourmets. The best I can describe pilaf is that it is an unusual rice that is half-cooked so that when you bite a grain it crumbles in your mouth and gives you that "starchy" taste that only comes from undone rice. Often, something on a gourmet plate comes on a "Bed of Pilaf." Boy, that's stretching things a bit.

Meat, But Precious Little

When it comes to the entree, sometimes it's a bit hard to spot on the plate. It may be something like two or three slight slices of pork tenderloin, a miniature piece of steak sometimes accompanied by a miniature piece of tough chicken breast.

Lobster is popular. Sometimes you may get a whole lobster tail if you are willing to spend enough. This is a contrast with people who get a whole lobster for less money in a non-gourmet restaurant. Then you may get something like Lobster Newburg if you want something a little less expensive. Lobster Newburg is where they may make somewhere between four and 14 servings by using just one lobster tail.

Fish is another favorite, but often a fish that you've never heard of. It, too, comes in slithers, or flakes, or very small pieces. Sometimes raw, sometimes almost raw. You see, the words WELL DONE are not in the gourmet vocabulary. Not when it comes to meat, fish, fowl or vegetables.

Whole, little birds of some kind may be on the menu. These "little" birds are probably the biggest gourmet portion you'll ever see. And this is the one case where the chef may approach the status of WELL DONE. But this is not a guarantee.

Sauces Are Big

There's usually an accompanying sauce of some kind. It may be on the vegetables or the meat or sometimes just spread over the plate. In this case, it may have a dollop or two of something with a contrasting color, squeezed out of a tube. This is usually to please your visual appetite. I personally never realized that my eyes were hungry. The types of food I eat taste the same whether you eat it with your eyes open or closed. The one exception might be boiled peanuts. You know the old saying, never eat boiled peanuts with your eyes closed.

Noodles are not unusual. Perhaps with gravy (I mean sauce) such as something like a clam puree or white sauce with a sprinkling of meat—you know, about as much as the 'chicken' in chicken noodle soup. Alfrado is one of the names I believe I've seen.

I have a theory for the reason so many sauces are called for in gourmet cooking, and it is not what you think the reason may be.

You see, gourmets are often kinda small people. They don't get a lot of food for their money, so they don't grow very much. Sauces are usually very rich. The reason for the sauce is to boost the caloric content of the meal so gourmets do get some nutritional value even with the small portions they encounter . . .

Value by Comparison

I like to figure out the number of bites in a gourmet meal and then divide that into the cost. That way you come up with an assigned monetary value to each bite.

If you check this out, you'll probably find that for perhaps two or three tiny bites of such gourmet delicacy, you could buy a whole meat and three vegetables meal (with really good sized portions), cornbread and/or a biscuit, in a regular country-cooking-type restaurant.

For about 1 3/4 to 2 1/4 bites, you could get a hamburger and fries. Chew twice more and you could enjoy a piece of apple pie with ice cream after the burger.

Perhaps I'm too frugal, or practical—you might even say cheap— to be able to enjoy gourmet food. I certainly don't need the sauce to boost the number of calories I normally eat at one sitting. Sauce to me means catchup (or catsup or ketchup) or maybe Texas Pete hot stuff, maybe even mushrooms in brown gravy to go on top of a hamburger steak.

Chapter 36

Status Symbols
My How They Change...

I never paid much attention to them, that is after I got out of high school. There are, however, two that stand out in my mind because they were mighty important to me back then.

One was to have a key chain that hooked to a belt loop and then proceeded to dangle down below pants pocket level before it curved back up to enter the bottom corner of the pocket.

Modeled somewhat after the old pocket watch chains but much longer, they came in gold or silver. They were used for things other than to hold keys. Sometimes you put a small knife on the end that went into the pocket, sometimes a watch, sometimes nothing. The real status came in how long the chain was and therefore how far down the side of your pants the loop went before it curved back up into the pocket. Some classmates attached the end clasp to the material just inside the pocket, thereby getting a longer loop because the end of the chain didn't go all the way to the bottom of the pocket.

The chain didn't have links, it was more like a metal rope. It was far more than just decoration. In times when you needed to be cool, you could pull it out and swing it in great arches around the index finger, eventually letting it coil around the finger in an ever-decreasing circle. It gave you something to do with your hands.

My other high school accomplishment was to be the proud possessor and wearer of the following outfit: charcoal gray pants, pink shirt, white tie, light gray sport coat and white shoes. I guess, for a while anyway, that was our official outfit of the period.

Modern Symbols

Today, I'm aware of two status symbol items that never cease to amaze me in the way they're carried and used.

First is the cellular telephone. How many times has someone pulled up beside you at a traffic light, glanced over to make sure you were looking, then picked up their cellular phone as though a call were coming in? Often, they'll smile as if to say: "Look what I've got. Do you have one?"

Portable phones are not new. I had one in my business car back in the early 1960s, but as I recall back then there were only two channels available and if they were both busy, you had to wait to place your call. But I didn't use mine to show off, although I must admit it was a bit exhilarating to be standing near my car talking business and all of a sudden have the horn start to blow.

"What's that?" they would say with a start, to which I'd answer, "Oh, that's just someone calling on my car phone."

A friend tells me about a businessman of somewhat questionable character here in Columbia who, when they first came out, had two installed in his car. When he came up beside someone at the light, he'd pick up both phones and put one to each ear. Now that's status!

Almost from the time the cellular craze hit, you could buy fake phones to impress people in other cars. Tell me this doesn't qualify as a status symbol.

The Latest Miracle Drink

The other status symbol of today is the plastic bottle of water. Oh, how impressive to be the only one to walk into a full-room business meeting bringing your very own bottle of water! Better yet, you walk in first, put your briefcase or notebook on the table at your chosen seat, and then place your bottle of water atop the stack. Then you leave the room, let the other people enter and all start to buzz and wonder who's the important person sitting in that seat!? Whereupon, you enter, take the seat, open the water and take a small sip. Proceed!

Walk through any large airport and you'll find people scurrying to their gate to board the plane while proudly waving around their plastic bottle of water. At the mall, watch the people coming out of the upscale shops. Count how many of them have their bottle of water.

In all cases, especially in the meeting room scenario, all the better if your particular brand of water has a red cap. It really stands out. Next most outstanding color is bright blue. I'd beware of white because it doesn't attract much attention. If you really prefer the taste, or price, of the water in the bottle with the white cap, buy a bottle which has a red cap, save the cap and switch it when you take the bottle which comes with white. You can use that cap for a long time if you rinse it occasionally in TAP WATER. Please be especially careful not to let any tap water drip into your container of extra pure bottled water! Realize, however, that your pure bottled water could well be tap water from another city.

Also noticeable is the way most people drink from a bottle of water. In days past when real people drank soft drinks from a glass bottle, they usually took a healthy SWIG. To consume bottled water in public where other people are sure to be watching, and be correct, you must not SWIG. Instead you SIP tiny little SIPS—almost non-perceptible SIPS. If you SWIG, the sides of the plastic bottle will collapse as you draw both air and liquid out of it. Then the bottle will make an uncool popping noise as air rushes back in to expand the bottle back to normal size before you recap it.

Another advantage of the SIP—I would be surprised if some of these bottles of water didn't last the present-day consumer a whole week or more. I guess it depends on how many meeting days you have in a week, and how many SIPS you feel obligated to take.

Let me caution new would-be status seekers of another rule. With the bottled water, as well as with the smallest-you-can-get cellular telephone, it is most important that these items be carried in plain sight. Never tuck them into a pocket, purse, brief case, backpack or cradle them in such a way in your hands and arms that they can't be seen by passers-by. You really defeat the whole purpose if no one knows that you really do have status because they can't see your symbols.

Others, of Course

There are, of course, other status symbols that are quite prevalent today, as my daughter reminds me, however, I have run out of space. We'll deal with these another time, but just to pique your interest I'll name a few:

Men: Suspender wearers who also wear a belt at the same time;

pierced ear devotees who, even though they only have two ears, have eight holes for ear rings; cutesy little pony tails; beer gut owners who wear the belt and waist of their pants just above the kneecap. They defy the laws of gravity and manage to keep their pants from falling off as everyone in the room gasps in awe at this magnificent accomplishment.

Women: Multi-pierced ear exhibitionist who may also sport a tongue or eyelid or belly button ring; joggers who abandon the sidewalk to run along the edge of the highway (saw one jogging down the median the other day); those who descend to the ridiculous on dress-down day at the office.

Chapter 37

Say it on the Bumper

I believe the first bumper sticker I ever saw read: SEE ROCK CITY. That probably dates me. Those were the days when people snuck around in parking lots at famous attractions, at ball games and other assorted places and put the stickers on the bumpers of unsuspecting and absent motorists. Very seldom did anyone put a sticker on their own car.

My Daddy hated bumper stickers. If anyone ever put one on our car, it became my task to try to scrub it off.

My how things have changed. Some people today even spend good money to buy a bumper sticker to go on their car. Today the purpose has expanded far beyond the original idea of a traveling advertisement. Bumper stickers can preach, espouse social positions, boost political ambitions, poke fun at traditions—you name it and there's a bumper sticker for it.

Here are a few of the favorites that I've seen through the years:

STAMP OUT TEXTILE IMPORTS (This one was on the bumper of a Toyota!)

THE WHOLE WORLD IS ON BACKORDER

SALES TAX IS A BIG WINNER: GOVERNMENT WINS, PEOPLE LOSE

ANYBODY BUT EARNHARDT

ANYBODY BUT GORDON

EVERY DAY IS SATURDAY (I'm Retired!)

THIS IS NEXT YEAR (In reference to USC Gamecocks Football)

The biggest bumper sticker I ever saw was not on a bumper, it was on a billboard. As I traveled through Georgia during the Jimmy Carter Administration, this sign stood near the small town of Plains. Remember Plains? The sign read:

THE REST OF THE PEANUT FARMERS OF GEORGIA APOLO-GIZE TO THE PEOPLE OF THE UNITED STATES.

Chapter 38

You Can Control the World by Remote Control

On my bedside table there are five remote control devices. There's one for the TV, one for the stereo, one for the CD player and two for two video recorders I have sitting on the television. It's not unusual for me to grab one and get upset when it doesn't work. Then I realize I have the wrong unit.

I know you can get what they call "universal" remote controls so you can put in a code for each device and use that one unit to control everything. My wife has one of those, but if you push the wrong button, it won't work until you put the correct code back into it. I always have to search for the instruction book when her unit messes up so I can look up the code again.

Sometimes soon I'll probably be able to click a button and set anything in the house in motion. Some people can do that already. I don't know whether I want any more remote control ability. I get precious little exercise as it is now. If I don't have to get up to make a cup of coffee or turn a light on in another room, then I'll get even less. By the way, we also have a lamp that all you have to do to turn it on is touch it. Touch it again and it gets brighter, again and it gets still brighter, again and it turns off.

Of course, every time the electricity flickers, that light turns on by itself. It's in a room where we don't go often, and unless I remember to check it when the house lights flicker, it turns itself on and stays on until someone goes into that room again. That's progress—right?

Cars That Toot and/or Beep

Lots of cars today come with remote control devices that will lock and unlock them, turn the headlights on and off—some people can even start their car by remote control.

I still jump every time I'm walking through a parking lot and a car I'm passing suddenly toots its horn, or beeps and clicks. I guess they do this when the owner does something or other with the remote device from across the lot.

I don't know about such things. Both of my cars and my pickup are old models. The only remote control device I have is the key and that's not very remote. I have to be right next to the door lock or the ignition to use the key.

My neighbor's carport is directly across from mine on the other side of the street. His car toots its horn or beeps all the time. Sometimes when it does, he comes out the house, gets in it and drives away. Sometimes he doesn't. I wonder if maybe, when the car beeps, it's calling him to say: "Let's go for a ride."

I used to remind people at shopping centers or office buildings or similar places that they had left their lights on. I did this until I got tired of them snootingly telling me that I shouldn't worry, the lights would turn off automatically. Now I don't take a chance on getting embarrassed. I just let all of them who walk off and leave the lights on, go right ahead and do so. I don't say a word. I do, however, secretly hope they have a model that turns them off all by itself. I know how bad it is to come away from an appointment, or a movie, or something like that and find out you've got a dead battery.

One Drawback

I've never seen a remote control device that works on only one battery. All of mine use two, my wife's uses three. If you multiply the cost of modern-day alkaline batteries by the number of remote controls we have, that can run into some money. The more expensive batteries are supposed to last longer. But you can buy several cheap batteries for what one good one will cost. Will the one good battery outlast three cheap ones? I don't know so I usually buy the cheap ones.

Fly That Airplane

I've often thought I'd like to try playing with one of those remote control airplanes. People who fly these things look like they're having such a good time. I've watched them, and even though they're enjoying themselves, you can tell from the expressions on their faces that they're really having to concentrate. They don't take their eyes off that craft.

It would be just my luck to have someone walk up and start talking, distract me. I'd probably turn for a second to look at them, then look back to the sky and not be able to find that tiny dot of airborne energy.

Wonder what happens when you lose sight of your airplane? How can you steer it if you don't know where it is? How can you land it? It doesn't know where home is. Can you imagine the panic when that happens. You could be dive bombing some car on the highway and not even know it. You could be inciting a riot in a nearby nursery school playground, or be chasing some high-heeled-business-suited woman down the sidewalk in front of the court house.

Nope . . . knowing my luck, I think I'll just watch other people having that kind of fun. I'll stick with just trying to pick out the right remote control off my bedside table so I can turn the TV off and go to sleep.

Chapter 39

The Expert Fisherman

I've always fancied myself as a pretty good fisherman. I've been doing it all my life, plus I've done an awful lot of reading and studying about the subject. Most people don't call it practicing, but that's what I did every time I got near the water. I was practicing to be a better angler.

Back in the 1970s, I even published an outdoor newspaper which came out every other week. The subject matter was fishing, hunting, boating, camping, hiking. I say I published it, actually there was a one-person staff and I was it.

I wrote 15 or 20 articles for each issue telling my readers what was biting, where it was biting, on which bait it was biting, how to catch it and what to do with it after you caught it. Got to interview many of the best professional anglers and fishing guides from all over the country. Manufacturers sent me lots of sample lures, especially their newest creations.

During this same time, I also fished some professional bass tournaments. Had one of those big boats with a big motor, lots of rods and reels, tackle boxes full of lures—every kind you can imagine.

I tell you this not to impress you, rather to set the stage for the person I'm getting ready to write about. He, too, had been fishing for many years—actually many more years than I had been living. I don't know whether or not he ever read any books or articles on the subject, but when he went fishing, he was consistent.

He did it his way. Regardless of what you, the boat owner and operator did, he did his kind of fishing. Didn't make any demands on you, didn't care what you were doing, never complained—just fished—his way.

Daddy Tom

The angler in question was my wife's Father—Thomas E. Wolfe. Everybody knew him as Daddy Tom.

I'll never forget the first time I took him fishing, or the last time I took him fishing, or any time in between those two memorable occasions.

I told him not to bother to bring any tackle—I had anything he could want to fish with. But he climbed aboard with the oldest, gray, metal tackle box I think I've ever seen. That and a matching ancient, bamboo fly rod.

"We're not going to be doing any fly fishing today, Daddy Tom," I told him.

"Whatever kind of fishing you want to do will be fine with me," he answered.

I was planning to cast for largemouth bass. "Don't you want to use one of my rods and reels?" I asked.

"No thanks, this one's fine," he said, stripping off the fly line and then taking it back up with the fly reel. He tied on a leader, then proceeded to add a hook and a split shot for weight. He pulled a can of earthworms out of his pocket and threaded one of the squirmies onto the hook.

"Oh," I mumbled, "I thought you were planning to fly fish."

"Don't have any," he answered.

"Don't have any what?"

"Flies."

"But you're using a fly rod. You mean you don't fish flies on a fly rod?"

To make a long story short, he never used a fly on that fly rod. He used earthworms, little spinners, small crank baits, top water lures. And he caught fish. You never knew what he was going to pull in—a crappie, bream, jack fish, catfish, bass.

On one trip when the bass weren't doing anything along the banks, I decided he might enjoy trolling. "I'm going to rig up one of my rods for you and maybe we can catch a striper trolling," I announced.

"No thanks," he said, "I'll stick with mine.

He rumbled though his tackle box and pulled out a six-inch purple worm that must have been one of the first ever invented. It was dirty and ragged and all crooked. Tied it on and let it trail only 12 or 15 feet behind the boat.

"I don't think you'll have much luck with that," I laughed as I tied on one of the latest crankbait deep runners. Before

I could get mine in the water, he was busy fighting a four-pound largemouth.

In the next 30 minutes, he boated two more only slightly smaller, while I had one strike, which I missed.

Trying not to be too obvious, I reeled in that fancy-colored crankbait and pulled out the oldest purple worm I could find and slipped it quietly into the water, not too far behind the boat. We brought home a good catch of fish that day—had some for supper and enough left over for several more meals.

After that, I had trouble in my mind figuring out who the real fishing expert was, but for the rest of the time we fished, I never did try to give him any more advice.

Chapter 40

My Very Own "R"

She's not quite as tall as a yardstick, has the bluest eyes you've ever seen, and her third birthday was celebrated a few months ago with squeals and laughter and blowing the candles out more than once.

She loves her Mom and her new baby sister most of all, her dog named Rabbit, doll babies everywhere and purple-anything purple.

She doesn't like chocolate, big boys at nursery who'll be mean to you, or bugs.

Her favorite activities include bubble baths, changing clothes several times a day, telling long and involved stories on the telephone and pumping gas into her play car.

Her friends include two different people at nursery named Jessica, everybody at a checkout counter in the grocery store who'll talk to her, and "Bebe," who sometimes is a boy and sometimes a girl. Adults have to be constantly on guard against sitting on Bebe because we've never been able to see this friend.

She's extremely proud of herself with each new thing she learns to do whether it's climbing up into the big pickup truck by herself, packing her own suitcase for a weekend visit, or tying her own shoes. She loves to demonstrate her skills and if she happens to be wearing shoes that fasten with Velcro, she'll quickly attack yours—untying them with a giggle and then redoing the bow in her own style.

She's quick to apologize when she thinks she's done something wrong like getting sticky candy on the car seat or falling down and hurting her knee when you told her to be careful walking down the steps. She's already discovered that the quickest way to end a scolding is to ask: "are you mad with me?" or "don't you love me anymore?"

She's not at all bashful about trying out new toys in the aisle at K-Mart, asking a stranger what their name is, or telling you she loves you.

She can say her alphabet but the only written letter she always recognizes is "R" and that's because her name is Rachael. She calls it her very own "R" and she lets you know with a shriek when she spots the capital version whether it's on a restaurant menu or the side of a truck or in a crowded department store. You'd better not lay claim to that "R" either, even if you have one in your very own name.

She's already decided that she wants to be a teacher when she gets big and she'll tell you right away that she'll be a good one. I believer her because she's already taught me a lot more about things I thought I was an expert on when her Mom was growing up.

She knows I love her, and maybe one day she'll even know that I'm trying hard to be a better Granddaddy that I was a Daddy. But right now she's content to play and learn and be happy, and in her words: "that's the bestest thing of all."

ORDER FORM

Use the order form below to obtain additional copies of this book.

Send your order to:

Larry Cribb
1900 Elm Abode
Columbia, SC 29210-7723

Please send _____ copies of *BACKYARD MEMORIES, FRONT PORCH DREAMS* @ $15.70 for each copy ($12.95 plus .75 sales tax plus $2.00 shipping/handling).

Amount Enclosed $_____

MAIL BOOKS TO: (*Please Print Your Name and Address*)

Name_____

Address _____

_____

City _____

State _____ Zip _____

DA
ORDER FORM

Use the order form below to obtain additional copies of this book.

Send your order to:

> **Larry Cribb**
> **1900 Elm Abode**
> **Columbia, SC 29210-7723**

Please send _____ copies of *BACKYARD MEMORIES, FRONT PORCH DREAMS* @ $15.70 for each copy ($12.95 plus .75 sales tax plus $2.00 shipping/handling).

Amount Enclosed $_____

MAIL BOOKS TO: (*Please Print Your Name and Address*)

Name _____

Address _____

_____

City _____

State _____ Zip _____